Creativity in Preaching

Books in this series . . .

THE CRAFT OF PREACHING SERIES

Creativity in Preaching

J. GRANT HOWARD

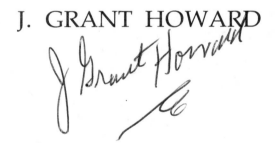

Special Edition for
Western Conservative Baptist
Theological Seminary

CREATIVITY IN PREACHING
Copyright © 1987 by J. Grant Howard

MINISTRY RESOURCES LIBRARY is an imprint of Zondervan Publishing House, 1415 Lake Drive, S.E., Grand Rapids, Michigan 49506.

Library of Congress Cataloging in Publication Data
Howard, J. Grant.
    Creativity in preaching.
    (The Craft of preaching series)
    Bibliography: p.
    1. Preaching. I. Title. II. Series.
BV4211.2.H69   1987   251   87-7907
ISBN 0-310-26251-8

The artwork on pages 104 and 106 is from the book *The Trauma of Transparency* by J. Grant Howard, copyright © 1979, and is used by permission of Multnomah Press.

All Scripture quotations, unless otherwise noted, are taken from the HOLY BIBLE: NEW INTERNATIONAL VERSION (North American Edition). Copyright © 1973, 1978, 1984, by the International Bible Society. Used by permission of Zondervan Bible Publishers.

Edited by Joseph Comanda
Designed by Louise Bauer

Printed in the United States of America

87 88 89 90 91 92 / CH / 10 9 8 7 6 5 4 3 2 1

To Howard Hendricks
My mentor
and a powerful model
for creative preaching

Contents

Preface

I love to preach, and I love to experiment. Put these two things together and you have a creative preacher. The following pages are designed to increase your love for preaching and to stimulate your willingness to experiment.

My thanks to Charlotte Lawrence for her expert work on the computer, and to Patty Wisner, Elizabeth Tucker, and Ruth Korch for their help with the graphics.

J. Grant Howard

1

The Components of Preaching

There are four essential elements in preaching: the text, the congregation, the preacher, and the act of preaching. Remove any one of these four and you no longer have the real thing. They constitute the irreducible minimum requirements if preaching is to take place. We identify them now for two reasons. First, they are foundational for any study of preaching. Even though they are well known, we dare not take them for granted. Familiarity breeds complacency, so right at the outset we reconfirm our commitment to the basics.

Second, this is a book on *creative* preaching, not on preaching per se. But creative preaching does not add to nor subtract from these four foundational factors; instead it seeks to utilize each one in legitimate, but new and different ways. So again at the very beginning we pledge to handle the basics with care . . . and . . . with creativity.

We can visualize the basics in the way shown in figure 1.1.

The task is to link the text and the congregation together. That happens when the preacher engages in the significant, fascinating work of preaching. It is his privilege to merge the truth of the text with the lives of his people. Why do we include both the preacher and his preaching in this center segment bridging the gap between text and congregation? Because communication of the Word of God involves a *person*—the *preacher*—and a *process*—*preaching*.

TEXT	PREACHER PREACHING	CONGREGATION

Figure 1.1

Let's face it, there are preachers who do poorly on the process, i.e., preachers who can't preach. By the same token, there is preaching that does poorly on the personal, i.e, preaching that doesn't relate. Effective preaching—listen up all you public purveyors of profound principles—takes place when the truth of the text works its way into the preacher, roaming through the corridors of his mind and heart, and then like a spring run-off after a winter of deep snow, it bursts over the spillway of his own life and plunges down into the minds and hearts of the congregation. The thirsty drink. The tired are refreshed. The dirty bathe. Then, as the rushing waters slow down they begin to form placid pools along the banks of one's life; mirrorlike surfaces that people can continue to gaze into, reflecting their needs, proposing God's solutions.

THE EXAMPLE OF PAUL

The Bible clearly and consistently recognizes all four of these ingredients in preaching. Paul, for example, identifies them for his young preaching protégé, Timothy, as we see in figure 1.2.

First, a word for the *preacher*. Plagued with the presence of false teachers (2 Tim. 3:13; 4:3–4) the preacher is exhorted to hang on to the truths he has learned and is convinced of.

Two reasons for such tenacity are offered. You know who shared them with you—your mother and your grandmother (1:5); and you know what they have done for you—given you wisdom that led to your salvation. So, as others have channeled this life-giving truth to you, reaffirm your commitment to the same task. Be a preacher who maintains a firm grip on the truth, and vice versa.

2 Timothy 3:14
"But as for you, continue in what you have learned and have become convinced of."

| TEXT | PREACHER

PREACHING | CONGREGATION |

2 Timothy 3:16	2 Timothy 4:2	2 Timothy 3:17
"All Scripture is God-breathed and is useful for teaching, rebuking, correcting and training in righteousness."	"Preach the Word; . . . correct, rebuke and encourage—with great patience and careful instruction."	". . . so that the man of God may be thoroughly equipped for every good work."

Figure 1.2

Next, a word about the *text*. It is conveyed through human channels, but it has a divine source. Every word of Scripture is sponsored by God and thus possesses unrivaled credentials for teaching, rebuking, correcting and training in righteousness.

These last four factors are not only nouns describing the text of inspired Scripture, but are also potential verbs ready to be employed in the act of preaching (cf. 2 Tim. 4:2).

In 2 Timothy 3:17 we skip over the bridge of preaching and go directly to the *congregation*. Where there is a preacher communicating the text, there will be people conforming to the text—a congregation populated with men and women of God "thoroughly equipped for every good work." The words of the text are designed to transform the lives of the people.

Finally, the *act of preaching*. A solemn charge in verse 2 tells Timothy what he is to do: Preach the Word. Four brisk imperatives follow in verse 2 explaining how to go about it. Be on standby, ready to proclaim anytime, anywhere. Be willing to correct, rebuke and encourage. Preaching is not composed of hesitant, hackneyed suggestions; it is bold, captivating communication that forcefully injects truth into life. Modifying these imperatives is the qualifying phrase "with great patience and careful instruction." That is because the preacher can lose patience with the erring brother who needs reproof. He may also omit the reasoned explanation from his fiery, impassioned exhortation.

There we have it—text, congregation, preacher, and preaching—succinctly presented and skillfully integrated in Paul's words to Timothy.

Autobiographically, Paul refers to these very same preaching components when he reminds the Thessalonians of the evangelistic ministry he and his team had among them.

> . . . because our gospel came to you not simply with words, but also with power, with the Holy Spirit and with deep conviction. You know how we lived among you for your sake (1 Thess. 1:5).

We can orient his words around our model in the fashion shown in figure 1.3.

The *text* is identified with one crisp term—*gospel*—the good news. The gospel *came* to them through the *act of preaching* which involved the use of words, but not simply with words. The spoken words were uttered with such power and conviction within each of the preachers that it could only have been generated by the Holy Spirit. Words only could be classified as monophonic communication. Words with Holy Spirit power and conviction would add a spiritual stereophonic depth and dimension to the act of preaching. It wasn't sterile audio. It was audible stereo.

"*our* gospel"

"how *we* lived"

TEXT	PREACHER PREACHING	CONGREGATION

"gospel"	"came"	"to you"
	"not simply with words, but also with power, with the Holy Spirit and with deep conviction"	"You know how we lived among you for your sake."

Figure 1.3

Note how the *preachers* are integrated into this process. It is *our* gospel, relating the preachers to the text. "You know how we lived among you for your sake"—calling attention to an intimate relationship between the preachers and the congregation. It is obvious each proclaimer had a truth-oriented relationship with the people.

In 1 Thessalonians 2:8 the apostle corroborates this personalized preaching style.

> We loved you so much that we were delighted to share with you not only the gospel of God but our lives as well, because you had become so dear to us.

The "gospel of God" is their text, highlighting both its source and its content. In 1:5 it was "our gospel," emphasizing the preachers' personal assimilation of the good news. "To share" describes the act of preaching; indicating a warm, personal touch. Now, don't miss the fact that the rest of the verse elaborates the relationship between the itinerate evangelists and the people in Thessalonica. It was an affectionate one, so much so that the preachers couldn't be content simply to distribute biblical data. They gave their own lives as well, meaning their total personalities were involved in transmitting the truth. This is holistic preaching. Preaching is not running truth through a pipe to a tank; it is filtering truth through a person to a person.

TESTING THE PRINCIPLE

Before we finish this chapter, I want you to try using this principle on your own. The model in figure 1.4 contains a passage of Scripture. Relate each part of the biblical text to the appropriate part of the model. The following discussion contains some questions to guide you.

In 5:18 what would "all this" relate to on the model?
Where would "who reconciled us to himself through Christ" fit?
Where would you put "gave us the ministry of reconciliation"?
Is there any particular significance to the use of the word "minister"?

In 5:19 where would you assign the first part of the verse, "that God was . . . against them?"
Is "he has committed to us the message of reconciliation" exactly parallel to the idea that he "gave us the ministry of reconciliation" in 5:18?

What will you do with the concept of "ambassadors" in 5:20?
Where does "making his appeal through us" go?
What is the significance of "we implore you"?

Finally, to which part of the model would you relate 5:21?

The Components of Preaching

Figure 1.4

2 Corinthians
5:18–21

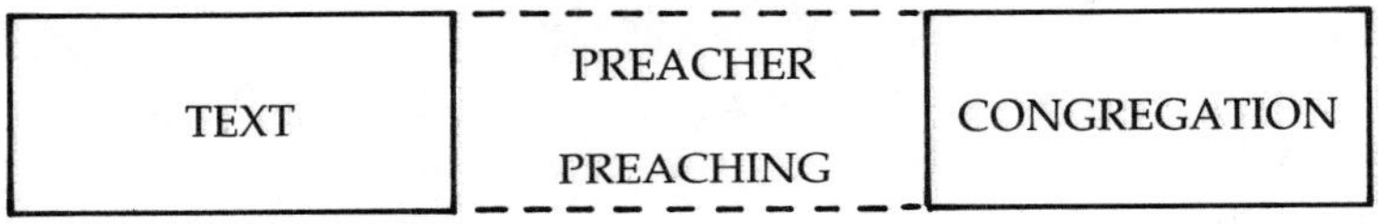

TEXT	PREACHER PREACHING	CONGREGATION

CREATIVITY IN PREACHING

There are a number of ways you could answer these questions. For some suggestions from the author, consult the endnote.[1]

SUMMARY

We can summarize this chapter with three brief statements. First, all four of the components of preaching are *important*. The Bible doesn't rank them in any particular order. Second, each of these preaching components is *different*. Those who preach must strive to master four unique areas. Third, all preachers must strive to keep these four ingredients in a healthy *balance*. Some tend to stress the text and the act of preaching. Others emphasize the preacher and the congregation. The Bible presents all of them in four-part harmony.

If *preaching* involves the text, the preacher, the act of preaching, and the congregation, then *creative preaching* must, of necessity, involve the very same factors. We will use the *text* creatively. We will engage in creative *acts of preaching*. As *preachers* our own experience and personalities will be creatively harnessed. The *congregation* will be educated and motivated to listen, learn, and respond *creatively*.

You see, it isn't that the preacher studies the text and prepares a sermon for his congregation and then adds a dash of creativity to be spicy and trendy. It isn't that at all. It is that the whole process, from text to congregation, can and should involve creativity. That is the flame this book wants to fan. But before we get into the how of doing this in detail, we need to understand what creativity is.

2

Creativity

GOD—THE CREATOR

To *create* is to bring into existence. To be able to create everything, one must be sovereign, omnipresent, omniscient, and omnipotent. Only God qualifies for this task. He alone reigns supreme, is everywhere, knows everything, and can do anything. Thus, He is the one and only Creator. Genesis 1–2 speaks eloquently to this fact. Therein we are informed that He created the world of nature and the world of human beings.

GOD—THE CREATIVE ONE

To be *creative* is to take the things that have been created and use them in new and different ways. In this sense, God is also the *Creative One*. For example, He created water, soil, and time. Then He used them creatively to fashion a Grand Canyon. He created color, air, clouds, and the sun. He combines these creatively for spectacular sunsets. He created a season we call "fall," wherein He bathes the green leaves in cold air, and the results are vivid hues that creatively expand the color spectrum. Then the leaves die and fall to the ground to creatively mulch the soil (or in the gutters to creatively clog the downspouts!).

God's creativity will always be in harmony with His character. He cannot creatively reorganize the Trinity, much less disband it. He cannot creatively redefine holiness, so that unsaved sinners could slip into heaven. But the self-imposed restrictions within the Godhead do not shut down or even hamper His creativity. There are an infinite number of ways that God can glorify Himself. He is not only the author of creativity; He is the epitome of creativity. His commentary on all that He created was that it was "very good" (Gen. 1:31). He could say that not only because of the quality of what He had created, but also because of the potentially unlimited quantity of ways it provided for Him to creatively express and exhibit Himself.

MAN—CREATOR OR "CREATIVE"?

What about man? Can he too be classified as a creator? No. As stated previously, to create is to bring into existence. Man cannot do that. Only God can. At the end of the sixth day God completed His work of creation, certified its intrinsic and supreme goodness, and took the next day off. Creation, for this life and in this world, is finished.

God is certainly not now an absentee God; He continues to be personally and dynamically involved: as Sustainer rather than Creator; as creative rather than creating.[1] But when God went into His creative and sustaining mode, man moved into his ruling and subduing mode. He had within him and around him all the potential resources he needed to carry out his God-given mandate. Now it was his responsibility, not to create (that had already been done), but to take the things that had been created and use them creatively. That would involve exploration, discovery, developing, combining, separating, testing—and a whole host of other procedures that constitute functioning creatively.

Creativity

MAN—THE CREATIVE ONE

I say it again. To be creative is to take the things that have been created and use them in new and different ways. The Garden of Eden was the setting for creativity at its highest level. The most creative couple in all human history were Adam and Eve. That was because Adam and Eve were doing everything *for the first time*. Every event was in a "start-up" phase as far as they were concerned. They had no prior experience. No textbooks. No owner's manuals. They undoubtedly consulted God, but they still had to discuss, understand, remember, and so on, and I have a sneaking suspicion that He didn't tell them all they wanted to know. He still doesn't (Deut. 29:29).[2]

Adam started his creative stewardship by naming the beasts of the field and birds of the air. God had created each one of them with a distinctive size, shape, color, movement, habitat, means of defense, and abilities. God had also created Adam with eyes to see, ears to hear, a mind to analyze, a mouth to form sounds. Adam had to put all these factors together and decide on a sound or sounds, depending on how many syllables or words he put in each name, for each bird and beast.

Note, Adam did not create the rich variety of animals. God did. Nor did Adam create his own capacity to form various sounds and words. God did. Adam, using what God had created in him and in the animals, creatively gave each a different name. He had no dictionary, no thesaurus, no name book. Working with the raw materials which God had already brought into existence he creatively fashioned a name. Then another name. And another; until all of the birds and the beasts were named. That little exercise, my friend, took a lot of creative thinking!

Everything was new and different for that first couple; so everything required some creative thinking and acting. What to eat, how to cook, where to sleep, how to engage in sexual relations, how to prune the trees, when to pick the fruit, etc., all demanded creative discussions and decisions.

Especially when they encountered these things for the first time.

I can just imagine Adam sighing deeply at the end of a busy day, and as the air rushed through his puckered lips, hearing for the first time—a whistle. Now what does one do with a whistle? Just what any growing child today does with such a discovery. Work on it. So Adam diligently practiced using his pulmonary potential creatively so as to produce all kinds of new sounds. He didn't stop there. He soon discovered that a low whistle with a certain flirtatious lilt to it turned Eve on, so he mastered that melody. By sticking two fingers in his mouth and blowing hard he could produce a sound shrill enough to get the cows headed for the barn, the kids headed for the supper table, the birds out of the yard, and the dog out of the chicken coop. All of this by creatively using his lungs and his lips.

Then Eve picked up on her husband's budding oral aerodynamic accomplishments and found that she had the knack of not only whistling little ditties, but also of putting appropriate words to the tunes. Then, on one occasion, when her lips were worn out from whistling, she discovered another way to make sounds—we call it humming. Their two boys also got in on the creative process. Abel found he could elicit a variety of sounds from an old ram's horn. Cain discovered the same thing while experimenting with a hollowed-out bamboo shoot.

The same creative process has continued down through the centuries, and today we have sophisticated wind instruments like the clarinet, oboe, flute, and bassoon; and no telling what some creative musician will come up with next. Certainly no one would be willing to say that we have in this area reached the end of our creative potential. That's the nature of God's creation—it has unlimited creative potential.

CREATIVITY AND THE FALL

Adam and Eve went on their merry way, creatively enjoying Eden and each other; carefully keeping the rules set up by their Creator. Then it happened. Seductively challenged by Satan to think incorrectly and to act disobediently, they wavered precipitously on the thin edge of decision and finally plunged headlong into the disastrous choice to pit their human wills against the will of their sovereign Creator. They sinned, and from that point on the world has been occupied by fallen, sinful human beings.

We know from Scripture and from experience that the Fall and the curse that followed profoundly affected man's *mind*. He can still think, but he can't always think *correctly*. Adam's mind began to malfunction immediately. He lost the proper perspective of nakedness. He tried to hide from God. He was slow to confess his active part in the forbidden indulgence. He tried to put the blame on his partner, Eve. His sons inherited this flawed thinking process, so much so that Cain came to the erroneous conclusion that the best way to solve a sibling squabble was to commit murder.

Within a few generations man's mind had deteriorated to the point where "every inclination of the thoughts of his heart was only evil all the time" (Gen. 6:5). Except for Noah's faithful remnant, the flood drowned out all of this bizarre thinking, yet before things hardly had time to dry out, God, knowing man's belligerent bent, instituted capital punishment (Gen. 9:5–6).

The world, the flesh and the devil continue to conspire to keep fallen people thinking half a bubble off plumb, at the very least. A classic analysis of man's cerebral corruption is contained in Ephesians 4:17–19:

> You must no longer live as the Gentiles do, in the futility of their thinking. They are darkened in their understanding and separated from the life of God because of the ignorance that is due to the hardening of their hearts. Having lost all sensitivity, they have given themselves over to sensuality so as to indulge in every kind of impurity, with a continual lust for more.

Notice the various descriptors used in this text that underline our basic premise: the natural person can't always think *correctly*.

But can they think *creatively?* Did the Fall lower their IQ? Granted someone may be afflicted with a satanic blindness; does that mean his mind is blank? To be sure, someone may be plagued with deceit; does that rule out discovery? Certainly he may be self-centered; does that rule out the ability to imagine and innovate? Not at all. Just because the natural person has problems thinking correctly does not mean that he is unable to think creatively.

Look again at Ephesians 4:17–19. Fallen folk are classified among other things, as ignorant and insensitive. But that doesn't shut them down. They have gone right ahead and committed themselves to "indulge in every kind of impurity, with a continual lust for more." They are not satisfied to be dull, narrow, traditional deviates. They sin creatively! This is reinforced in Romans 1:28–32 where those with depraved minds are said to "invent ways of doing evil."

This does not mean, however, that non-Christians spend all of their time thinking and acting immorally. As Richard Lovelace points out, "their lives may be more righteous in outward actions, though not in motivation, than those of most Christians." Their basic motivation, Lovelace says, "may simply be to hang on to respectability, a need based on the desire for self-esteem and the affection of others."[3]

Another basic motivation in the non-Christian world is the desire to make life better. Technology is designed to do that. So is secular humanism. Creative thinking has spawned technology. Correct thinking is now needed to make sure we use it rightly. Incorrect thinking has given rise to secular humanism, and now creative marketing is being used to sell it to the masses; a quick look around us at magazines and television demonstrates how it's happening. The Christian communicator must step boldly into this scene and market correctly and creatively the insights needed to handle technology and the antidote needed to counteract secular humanism. Creative biblical preaching is one of the significant ways to accomplish this.

CREATIVITY AND THE CHRISTIAN

The preceding section established the fact that the unsaved person has both the propensity to think incorrectly and the potential to think creatively. We must not let this lead us to the erroneous conclusion that because the saved person now has the potential to think correctly, there is no reason to worry about thinking creatively. Correct thinking neither rules out nor replaces creative thinking. Both are mandatory for the Christian.

Scripture weaves correctness and creativity together. For example, in Romans 12:2 the renewing of the mind is viewed as basic to everything else in the verse. It enables the believer to think and live correctly with regard to conformity to the world, and it will give him the ability to test and approve with accuracy what God's will is in life situations. Where is creativity in this passage? It is inherent in the exhortation to "be transformed." To be transformed is to change, to be different, to be new. This happens as we allow the Spirit of God to blend His pervasive truth into our unique personalities. The result: a custom-made Christian. Not another one in all this world exactly like him. Creativity at its highest!

These same two factors are laced together in 1 Corinthians 15:58. Correctness is emphasized in the two phrases "stand firm" and "let nothing move you." As the Christian lives life and faces death he needs to be unshakably rooted in God and His Word. But there is more. Along with a correct rootedness, there is to be a creative flowering, described as "always giving yourselves fully to the work of the Lord." The NASB translates this as "always abounding in the work of the Lord." There are an infinite number of ways we can give ourselves fully to the task of abounding, especially when we understand that none of our labor will be in vain.

Paul's philosophy of evangelism combined correctness and creativity. Five times in 1 Corinthians 9:19–23 he reiterates his goal—to win others to Christ. Most assuredly, that is a correct goal. It never changes. Paul's methods, however, frequently changed, for he creatively adapted his approach to the nature and needs of his audience. He summarized his innovative ministry by saying, "I have become all things to all men so that by all possible means I might save some."

Note the use of the word *all*. "All things . . . all men . . . all possible means." It is a little word, but it has big implications. While there is *one reason* to do evangelism, there are *many ways* to do it. The apostle was committed to creative outreach.

First Corinthians 10:31 is a good verse with which to close this section. "So whether you eat or drink or whatever you do, do it all for the glory of God." The "glory of God" is the essential correctness factor here. His "glory" refers to His character—namely, all that is true of God. All that we do needs to be monitored by and expressive of the glory of God. Notice how the verse moves from the specific—"whether you eat or drink"—to the general—"or whatever you do." Then comes that little word "all." We could classify it as a *creative* "all," rather than a *restrictive* "all." These are words of challenge, expansion, exploration, imagination, innovation, variation, invention.

All that we do needs to be carefully analyzed to be sure that it conforms to His character, but having done this, we still have an "all" that is larger than anything we can imagine. So when you preach, do it "all" for the glory of God. Realize when you take this approach there will be some things you would never say and do when you preach, but having put these away, you will still have an unlimited number of ways you can preach and in so doing bring glory to God.

CREATIVITY AND COMPETENCY

We are using the term *creativity* in a broad, general, nontechnical sense. You will remember we defined it earlier in this chapter as "the ability to take the things that have been created and use them in new and different ways."

Creativity

Using this definition, creativity can include such things as innovation, imagination, invention, variety, originality, and technique. Each of these terms can have qualities which would distinguish it from others on the list, but they can also be used in ways that make them essentially synonymous. For the most part, we will employ them in this latter way, and we will use *creativity* as a broad umbrella term that covers all the others.

Anyone can be creative. This is because anyone can put the above definition of creativity into effect, i.e., he can take something that exists and use it in a new and different way. Furthermore, since every Christian is expected to glorify God in and through his unique personality, and thus creatively, we can rightly conclude that every Christian is able to do so. There are no noncreative persons. There are, however, many persons who have not discovered or who are not using areas of creative potential in their lives. This book is not written to a select few whom God has equipped to be creative. The author's assumption is that every believer has the potential to be creative and simply needs to discover and develop it.

Gifts and *talents* are given to us by God. Talents are bestowed by God at conception. Gifts are bestowed by God at conversion. Talents enable us to function primarily in the world. Gifts enable us to function primarily in the church. Talents are related more to our vocation; gifts are related more to our ministry. Both talents and gifts are inherent capacities as opposed to learned abilities. Therefore, our task is to discover what specific capacities we inherently possess, rather than decide what particular abilities we want to acquire. We should be able to think and act more skillfully in areas where we are gifted and talented, for these are our God-given places of strength and expertise, places where we can perform exceedingly well. It is in these areas that we will be most creative—uniquely qualified—to put things together in new and different ways. Because no one person has all the gifts and talents, no one person will be skillful and creative in every area of endeavor. That underscores the doctrine of interdependency. We need one another's creative skills.

From a biblical perspective, *competency* can be viewed at three levels. A Christian would be functioning *below* biblical competency when ignorant and/or disobedient with regard to God's will in one or more areas of life. That was the problem with the Hebrew Christians (Heb. 5:11–14). Enough time had elapsed for them to be teachers; but because of ignorance and disobedience they weren't there. They needed to be retaught the basics. With regard to teaching the Word to others, they were wallowing around in an area we are classifying as below biblical competency. Any creativity they may have had was probably being used to find new and different ways to avoid their God-given responsibilities!

A second level can be called *within* biblical competency. That's where the Hebrew Christians should have been. The indictment leveled at them was candid: "by this time you ought to be teachers." They should have been competently communicating truth to others. In contrast, note how Paul commends the Christians in Rome for their progress with these words:

> I myself am convinced, my brothers, that you yourselves are full of goodness, complete in knowledge and competent to instruct one another (Rom. 15:14).

These believers were within biblical competency in at least three areas: goodness, knowledge, and instruction. The better they got, the more the potential for them to creatively function in these three areas. Note, however, that neither Hebrews 5:11–14 nor Romans 15:14 contains a reference to the spiritual gift of teaching. These passages refer to the ministry of teaching that any believer can and should be competent to carry out.

To account for the presence and use of spiritual gifts and talents, there must be one higher level of competency, which I have chosen to call *skill*. The person with the *gift of teaching* will be able to teach the Word of God exceedingly well, i.e., with skill. The person with *artistic talent* will be able to employ that talent with expertise. If a preacher has the gift of teaching and an artistic talent, then his preaching can and should combine these two capacities creatively.

Now, a word about *talents.* One talent is that of *communication.* It involves the inherent capacity to write, or converse, or to broadcast. If you have the gift of teaching and the talent of using words, you will be able to creatively verbalize the Word of God. You will do it because you have a knack for it, and when you do it, you experience a growing sense of fulfillment—because you are doing "your thing." Or better, God is doing "His thing" in and through you. But your word-using talent may be in the field of writing and thus you minister through the print media, or you manuscript your sermons and utilize your writing talent orally.

CREATIVITY AND CHANGE

Roots become ruts. Ruts become routines. Routine, carried on in the local church, tends to become "righteous." Righteous routine becomes unassailably, uncritically rigid— the best and only way to do things. Along come those who want to make a change in this rigidly righteous routine. They may find out that what they propose to change is something that others are deeply attached to and not about to change. So, to get to the point, not everyone in the local church is going to appreciate your desire to be creative, especially when you attempt to be creative in your preaching. Fierce defenders of the established faith are also often fierce defenders of the established format.

The solution is not to write them off and run over them, nor is it to let them run over you. The solution is to help people distinguish between biblical doctrines and historical practices. Doctrines we change only in order to become more biblical. Preaching is a vital part of a biblical ministry. That's a doctrine we ought to be unalterably attached to. Practices we change in order to become more effective in our biblical ministry. Thus, we hold firmly not only to the primacy of preaching but also to the ongoing development of effective preaching. This allows us, nay, compels us, to look for, find and use new and different and better ways of communicating God's Word from the pulpit. This demands creativity. With regard to biblical doctrine we are firm. With regard to historical practices we are flexible. The rest of this book is going to test how flexible you really are.

3

Creatively Re-Creating the Life-Setting of the Text

Every text of Scripture has a context, or an original setting, or what I call a *life-setting*. To discover the meaning, we study the text in its life-setting. Some factors in this are culture, history, geography, thought, feelings, language, grammar, names, and persons. Using these elements and a sound hermeneutical system, the expositor seeks to step back into both the time and the territory of the text.

Studying the text in its life-setting is important, for Scripture is more than words on paper; Scripture is people. In one sense the Bible is a script as for a drama. Our task is to re-create each scene, to identify the players and bring them onto the stage, to let them play their parts. To accomplish this we must fervently study the text *and* frequently use our imagination. Let's do it.

LIFE-SETTING AND LANGUAGE

Suppose you are *speaking* to a live audience and want to emphasize one main point. How do you go about this? You establish eye contact, use appropriate gestures, carefully vary the volume and rate of your voice, and use effective words. Suppose you are *writing* rather than speaking. For emphasis you might use italics, underlines, bold-faced type, capital letters, quotation marks, graphics, or indentation, along with carefully selected words.

Suppose you were doing this writing in the *first century* A.D. What options for emphasis would you have? We can find out by examining a writer like the apostle Paul to see how he emphasized a major point. Let's work with a well-known passage from the pastoral epistles.

> All Scripture is God-breathed and is useful for teaching, rebuking, correcting and training in righteousness, so that the man of God may be thoroughly equipped for every good work (2 Timothy 3:16–17).

In verse 16 Paul tells Timothy about the source and the use of the Scriptures. They are "God-breathed" and thus essential "for teaching, rebuking, correcting and training in righteousness." The overall purpose of these uses of Scripture is given in the *hina* clause in verse 17: "so that the man of God may be thoroughly equipped for every good work." The apostle's main point is this: The Scriptures equip believers.

How does Paul establish this emphasis? He couldn't write louder, or send a videotape. He didn't choose to write larger, or use all capitals, or underline, or change the color of his ink, or use a broader-pointed quill. What did he do to drive home this basic truth? As we carry on this investigation, bear in mind that we are exploring what we might call the linguistic life-setting of Paul—finding out how he used words to forcefully invade people's lives.

The phrase "thoroughly equipped" needs our attention. It is the translation of two similar Greek words. First, the noun *artios*, which means "equipped, ready, prepared." The Word of God is designed to *equip* the man of God. However, the phrase says "thoroughly equipped." That is because in this verse there is a second, similar word, *exertismenos*, which is a verb derived from the noun *artios*. It is a perfect passive participle, used to describe an action that has taken place in the past, the results of which continue into the present.[1] Again, it is the Scriptures which will *completely equip* the man of God with insight about every good work. The Scriptures started this work at a point in the past—in Timothy's case, infancy (3:15)—and continue it till now. Biblical equipping can and should be a lifelong process.

Do you see what is happening? To forcefully underscore the purpose clause in verse 17, the writer repeats himself, employing the word *equipped* twice in the same verse. That's a good way to emphasize. But he is doing more than writing the same word twice. He attaches a prefix to the second word. It is the preposition *ex*, which is used here to emphasize and intensify the word; thus the translation "thoroughly equipped."[2] The New International Version seeks to capture the impact of both these words in a single phrase, but in actuality these two words for "equipped" do not occur next to each other in the verse. The basic word is at the beginning, and the intensified word is at the end. A more accurate translation of the Greek text would be: "so that *equipped* may be the man of God, for every good work he has been, and will continue to be, *thoroughly equipped*."

Led by the Spirit of God, Paul has chosen certain words and put them together in a certain way.

- He uses selection—picking out a choice word from his vocabulary to convey the concept of equipping;
- He uses repetition—to give them a double dose of equipping;
- He uses a noun and its verb form—to feature both the product and the process of equipping;
- He uses the perfect tense—to underline the ongoing effectiveness of equipping;
- He uses a prepositional prefix—to intensify the significance of equipping;
- He uses positioning—fore and aft—to remind us coming and going about equipping.

Why did Paul use all these highlighting techniques? Because he ardently believed that the *Word equips Christians,* and he wanted to convey that commitment to Timothy, expecting him in turn to convey it to others (2 Tim. 2:2).

So we have more than a set of exegetical facts in front of us. We have insight into the life of the human author. Knowing how he put verse 17 together, we are gripped by his confidence in the Word and by his concern for equipping. If you want to preach this passage powerfully and creatively, get so close to the text that you rub shoulders with the author and his confidence and concern work their way into your life.

You may want to use your imagination and develop a conversation Paul could have had with himself as he prepared to write this verse, sifting through the different means he might use to get his point across, and finally discovering what was to him (and the Spirit) the best way to communicate to Timothy the concept of "equipping." Don't be afraid to do this, because the fact is that Paul no doubt did mull various options over in his mind before and as he was writing. We certainly do it, and Paul was no less human than we are. That's one way of creatively re-creating the life-setting of the text.

If you want to do the same kind of things in other texts, look for repetition of key words—sometimes the same word, sometimes a synonym. Look for the prepositional prefixes, especially those that amplify and intensify.

At this point I suspect that you would like me to give you a list of other passages of Scripture which have interesting uses of repetition and intensification. I prefer to challenge you to look for these kinds of factors in the texts from which you choose to preach. However, I have provided a few ideas in a note at the back of this book.[3]

LIFE-SETTING AND HISTORY/CULTURE

Now that we have sharpened our linguistic sensitivity a bit, let's vitalize our historical-cultural awareness. Every portion of Scripture was formulated in a particular historical-cultural setting, meaning that it was written at a certain time in history, written in a certain place, and involved certain people. Time is history, place is culture, and people are germane to both. The more we can re-create this original life-setting, the better we can understand and transmit the truth formulated in it. I will show you what I mean.

Who wrote the Epistle to the Romans? Paul. In one sense. A man named Tertius actually wrote down the words (16:22). So there were two people vitally involved in the production of the original manuscript. Probably others.

Why do I say this? In Romans 16:23 we are introduced to Gaius, owner of the house where Paul stayed during his three months in Corinth. As a matter of fact, the entire Corinthian church enjoyed Gaius' hospitality on occasion. So if Gaius lived there, and Paul and Tertius stayed there and composed the letter to the Romans there, then Gaius no doubt listened in now and then, asked a question once in a while, and perhaps even offered suggestions.

These men were close friends, you know; Gaius was one of the few believers whom Paul himself baptized. Gaius, his wife, and their servants surely provided meals for Paul and Tertius, along with mid-morning and mid-afternoon "coffee breaks." I can imagine that during these lighter moments the conversation included politics, business, sports, and the weather in Corinth, *as well as* the imputation of sin, justification by faith, being more than conquerors, God's sovereignty, Israel's future, spiritual gifts, responsibilities of citizenship, the gray areas of life, etc., depending on where they were in the letter to the Romans that particular day. I can't conceive of Paul and Tertius shutting themselves up in a room for twelve hours every day, having their food slipped under the door, not engaging in any small talk with each other, or refusing to discuss the nature and progress of their long, important letter with anyone else because it was "top secret." I feel certain, also, that Erastus and Quartus dropped by frequently and got involved in numerous discussions with Paul and his friends about life in general and the letter to the Romans in particular (16:23). The same goes for Timothy, Lucius, Jason, and Sosipater (16:21).

CREATIVITY IN PREACHING

These incidents and conversations *could have happened.* The text doesn't say that they did, but given the presence of the individuals mentioned in Romans 16:21–23, it is certainly not wrong to assume that a lot of interpersonal interaction took place. So, in the absence of any "Corinthian Cassette Tapes," let's use our imagination with regard to some of the things that might have happened.

Erastus was a prominent figure in Corinth—the city treasurer no less. When you preach Romans 13:1–7, bring him into a conversation with Paul about civil government and, more specifically, taxes. Quartus is described simply as "our brother." While writing Romans 12:10 Paul might have asked Tertius who had been there that morning who exemplified this truth. Tertius might have quickly identified Quartus, giving a practical example of his brotherly love, and then commenting on the fact that it was unusual for the youngest of four brothers (Quartus = "fourth") to be so mature in loving interpersonal relations, or perhaps it was the powerful, positive modeling of his three older brothers that produced it. Or perhaps he was an only child born on the fourth day of the month and his parents provided him with a positive example.

These are the kinds of things you can do to creatively re-create the life-setting of the text. At times, listening to an exposition of Scripture is about as exciting as watching house paint dry. Add a dash of color to your communication of the Word. You can be faithful to the text and still use your imagination.

Spirited interaction between Paul and Tertius probably went on frequently during the writing of Romans. To visualize Paul as an aloof, impersonal purveyor of prosaic, cold facts, and Tertius as a passive, shallow, receiver of these facts is unrealistic. Belief in the "God-breathedness" of the Word does not require us to rule out human relations between composer and secretary. We do not have to sacrifice the human personalities of Paul and Tertius on the altar of inspiration. Let's creatively re-create what might have happened in the development of Romans 12:2.

Creatively Re-Creating the Life-Setting of the Text

The time: Friday evening, about 9:30.

The place: Corinth, at Gaius' large, comfortable home in the suburbs.

The people: Paul and Tertius. Erastus got free tickets, and he and the rest of the household are off to the Isthmian Games being held at the Corinthian Coliseum. Except for Jason, Sosipater, and Timothy—it's their night to bowl in the Corinthian Christian League.

The room: An enclosed porch off the living room. The floor is made of large slabs of limestone. The roof is constructed of large beams fairly close together, with reeds and bushes laid on top and a hard clay over these. The walls are mud bricks. The wooden doors on the windows are wide open this fall evening, with a lattice-work wooden screen that gives some privacy and admits the cool breeze. The doors are made of heavy sycamore, sagging a bit on the heavy iron hinges.

The furnishings: An oil lamp on the corner table; another one on the desk, where Tertius writes on sheets of papyrus with his quill and ink. A stool in the corner, a couch against the wall, and plenty of room in the middle for Paul to ponder and pace back and forth as he formulates the Spirit-inspired letter to the believers in Rome.

That sets the scene. Now we open the curtains and listen to a dialogue between Paul and Tertius.

Paul pauses for a moment, then slowly adds four more words: *"to thelema tou theou."*

" 'The will of God.' Ah! I am beginning to see what you are driving at, Paul. As our minds are renewed by the Scriptures, we are being equipped to figure out for ourselves in various life situations what the will of God is. That's a great concept, Paul. The people in Rome should appreciate it. I know I sure do. Okay, that's enough! It's late. Can we put a period there and quit till tomorrow morning? I'm getting writer's cramp.''

The stocky apostle stood motionless, meditating. Then, driving a clenched fist into the palm of his hand, he blurted, "No, Tertius, we can't stop yet! This is the first time in this letter that I've used 'the will of God' in this way. It's too important to leave it dangling there on its own. We need to add something.''

"Well, . . . okay . . . but could we make it quick? I can hardly focus on the papyrus, my eyes are so tired.''

"Mine, too . . . now what we need is an adjective that will capture the nature of the will of God. How could we do this? . . . yes . . . here . . . write this down . . . *to agathon*.''

" '*To agathon*' it is. Why this word, Paul?''

"Because it signifies that which is morally good in relation to God. I might have used *kalos*, but sometimes it has the idea of aesthetic beauty.''

"And what you are saying is that the will of God for the believer will always be that which is essentially good.''

"Exactly . . . as opposed to that which is bad.''

"The oil is getting low in the lamp. Can we call it a day?''

"Can't stop now, Tertius! People may tend to think that the will of God is primarily 'list living'—slavish obedience to things that are right, rejection of things that are wrong. It *is* that, but it is *more* than that.''

"I see your point, but . . .''

"*Euareston*. Write it down, Tertius, my boy.''

Creatively Re-Creating the Life-Setting of the Text

"Not sure I know how to spell it . . ."

"*E-u-a-r-e-s-t-o-n*. You know this word. Often used in a family context with reference to the obedient child. He or she is *euareston* —pleasing to his parents." A brief pause, then with a twinkle in his eye, Paul mused, "Maybe your father didn't use it very often with regard to your behavior when you were growing up!"

"I guess not. I was pretty wild in my younger years."

"Well, let me tell you something very interesting about this word. The other day I was reading in the Greek translation of the Hebrew Scriptures—you know, the Septuagint—and early in Genesis [5:22] the Hebrew text says that 'Enoch walked with God.' Guess how they translated 'walked'? '*Euareston.*' Enoch was 'pleasing' to God."

"Now you've got my juices flowing, Paul. The last time I was in Jerusalem I attended a symposium on the sayings of Christ, and I clearly recall the apostle John quoting Christ as saying that He always did that which was 'pleasing' to His heavenly Father."

"See how one little word helps, Tertius? Do the will of God, and you will be engaged in a lifestyle pleasing to Him."

"And if you are pleasing God, you would no doubt be pleasing your parents, and your boss, even your pastor."

"Precisely! And when one is disappointing his parents, he is probably disappointing God. See what I am driving at? I want them to have a concept of the will of God that is personal, as well as propositional."

"Right! . . . All kidding aside, Paul, I am really wiped out! It would be pleasing to me if we could end it right here."

"Stay with me, Tertius! Every sermon needs three points. Let me give you one more adjective to shed additional light on the meaning of 'the will of God.' "

"Okay! But make it quick, or we are going to need more oil to shed light on the manuscript."

"*Teleion.*"

"*T-e-l-e-i-o-n,* meaning . . . don't tell me . . . 'mature, grown up.' "

"Absolutely! The will of God will always be the mature attitude. The grown-up action."

"And the opposite approach to life is to think and act immaturely, like a baby. I think I performed like that the other day when I got so frustrated at not being able to find my sandals, and even went to the point of accusing Timothy of taking them."

"Good insight, Tertius. Shows you are growing. . . . All right, we are through for the day. Sleep in a bit tomorrow, if you want to. We won't start till seven o'clock!"

Through an imaginative dialogue that could have happened, we have developed what might be part or even all of a sermon on three adjectives that are used to describe the nature of the will of God. Paul didn't have to use any descriptive words, but he chose to. He didn't have to use three, but he chose to. He didn't have to use these three, but he chose to. He didn't have to use Tertius, but he chose to. He did all these things with meaning and purpose.

What we are seeking to do is capture the meaning and purpose of the text through the creative medium of a dialogue, a dialogue that well might have occurred. Even if it didn't occur as we have imagined, as long as there is nothing false or misleading in the conversation we have designed, it is certainly a legitimate method of communicating the truth of the text.

This kind of dialogue can be done anywhere in Romans, or in any other portion of Scripture where a scribe and the author were functioning together. It could be done as a dramatic monologue, with one person speaking both parts; or two people doing it "live"; or prerecorded and played through the sound system as part of the sermon; or done with the preacher having a dialogue with an offstage, live, voice through the sound system. The preacher could play one or both roles, or he could turn it over to other staff members, or enlist the services of qualified laypeople in the congregation.

Our sample from Romans could be expanded into a whole sermon, or condensed to be just a brief illustration, and/or the dialogue could be carried on into the realm of personal, practical application. Gaius and Sosipater could arrive on the scene and get involved in the discussion. Regardless of how it is developed and delivered, don't lose sight of the fact that the purpose is to creatively re-create the life-setting of the text and, in so doing, to expound the text with added historical, cultural, personal, and interpersonal dimensions.

We turn to the Old Testament to illustrate another way of capturing the historical-cultural life-setting of the text. In the Book of Ecclesiastes, Solomon is probably delivering a series of insightful fireside chats to the older and younger members of his court. In 7:13–14 he relates God to the good and bad, straight and crooked experiences of life. This brief, inspired, literary vignette on the sovereignty of God had some kind of life-setting. It might have been something like this:

The sun sank slowly into the Mediterranean, bathing the temple buildings in a warm, red glow. It was about seven o'clock when Solomon wheeled his chariot into the palace parking lot and headed for his reserved spot near the buildings. His weekly meeting with his Cabinet and other leaders in the nation Israel was scheduled for 7:30 on this Thursday evening. As the king stepped down from his chariot, he paused to wait for Tony, who had just pulled in alongside him.

"Hi there, Tony! Had a good day?"

"Not really! Terrible, as a matter of fact."

"What happened?"

"Well, I've been up with my little boy, Ebenezer, since three this morning. I think he has the Babylonian flu. It's been going around the neighborhood. Then on the way to work, my right chariot wheel fell off and I sprained my back getting it on. That meant I got to work about an hour and a half late.

"And wouldn't you know it—the camel caravan due in from Damascus at noon was over four hours late. I desperately needed that shipment of Moab miniskirts and Assyrian socket wrenches this morning.

"Finally, I got home and was relaxing in the front room and guess what—the paper boy threw the *Jerusalem Journal* right through the front window. And may I remind you—we take the Sandstone edition. What a mess! To top it off, while we were all cleaning up the living room, Claudia's supper burned to a crisp and we ended up eating leftover, cold Chaldean casserole.

"All in all, it has been a terrible, horrible, no-good, very bad day!"

"What a day! How do you handle all those unexpected, unwelcome events?"

"I don't know. Sometimes I try and figure out how I could have planned ahead to avoid the interruptions. Sometimes I get good and mad. Sometimes I just give up, passively resigning myself to the fact of fate—that's the way life is."

"Let's go inside, Tony, the meeting is about to start. Listen carefully! What I have to say should help you work your way through these kinds of days."

Creatively Re-Creating the Life-Setting of the Text

We can sit in on this message too, because it is recorded for us in Ecclesiastes 7:13–14. Tony was the figment of my imagination. But there could have been a Tony in Solomon's court, and he could have had a bad day, and he could have been there when these concepts were presented. Furthermore, there could well have been some humor in Tony's experience. Life is funny as well as serious, and our preaching should reflect this balance. The introduction we have suggested contains a brief dialogue of humorous realism—realism that would pave the way for a careful exposition of two verses that deal profoundly and and practically with the doctrine of the sovereignty of God.

You might bring Tony onto the platform live and interview him. You might get two laymen or staff and have them present this in skit format at the beginning of the message. Or Tony could be interviewed at the close of the sermon to see how he is going to apply these truths in the future. Tony's wife, Claudia, could also be a part of any of these scenes, as could his young children or teenagers. Tony could be a seasoned saint or a brand-new believer. Use your imagination! Make the Scriptures come alive!

INNER-LIFE-SETTING

To this point we have dealt with life-settings as they relate to certain aspects of language, history, and culture. Our approach has been primarily interpersonal. But there is also an *intrapersonal* aspect—that is, what goes on within the person. For example, Jesus told the disciples his heart was troubled as he contemplated the agony of the cross (John 12:27). Paul revealed to the Romans his perpetual sorrow and anguish over his unsaved brethren in Israel (9:1–5). In the parable of the Prodigal Son, we know what the young man said to himself when he came to his senses in the pigpen (Luke 15:17–19). In the Psalms we are frequently given insight about the inner state of the author, as in Psalm 43:5. However, there are many portions of Scripture where what is going on inside the individual is not explicitly revealed, yet it would aid our interpretation and application of the text if we knew what the person was thinking and feeling. That's where we bring our imagination into play. That's where we creatively re-create the life-setting and then probe the inner recesses of the individual(s) involved in the text. What was he thinking? How was she reacting? How do they feel about that? Why did he say that? Why did she do that? Asking and answering such questions will enable us to discover and develop the inner-life-setting of the text.

Actually, we have already done some of this internal investigation. We have seen how strongly Paul felt about the "equipping" nature of the Word. We have thought along with him as he mentally decided on three adjectives to amplify the meaning of the will of God. We have tried to read the mind of a tired Tertius. We have suggested a possible incident that might have caused Solomon to arrange his thoughts as presented to us in Ecclesiastes 7:13–14.

Peter offers us plenty of inner-life data. Let's do some perceptive peeking inside this often impetuous man. In Matthew 16:13–15, Jesus moved from a general question, "Who do people say the Son of Man is?" to a specific question, "Who do you say I am?"

How would you compare the internal pressure on the disciples with reference to these two questions? The second involves more pressure because it is more personalized and thus more threatening. Right? So you might profitably analyze Christ's purpose in going from the general to the specific with His disciples. You could also seek to crawl inside the mind of one or more of the disciples and figure out what kind of a trip his ego was taking at that moment. Was he soaring with insight, or searching for identity?

Peter comes up with the answer, "You are the Christ, the Son of the living God" (16:16). When? After a period of awkward silence, or quickly before any of his colleagues had time to respond? Why? To show them up, or to help them out? Was he their recognized spokesman, or a self-appointed know-it-all? Was he a quick thinker, or a pushy egotist? Was he trying to *get* on top, or *stay* on top? These are the kinds of questions that will help us understand the inner-life-setting of this text.

In Matthew 16:17–19 Jesus gives words of praise and affirmation to Peter, but makes it quite clear that Peter hadn't come to his correct conclusion about who Christ was on his own; this truth was revealed to him by the Father in heaven. I wonder if Peter heard these latter facts. I wonder if the "blessed are you" was booming away, over and over in his mind, essentially drowning out everything else the Lord had to say. In my own experience I find it tempting to replay affirmation tapes over and over, letting them inflate my fragile ego, possibly blocking out other needed insights. When we do well and people praise us, watch out. At the point of praise we become very vulnerable.

One of the main reasons why we sense that Peter was majoring on himself is what happened in Matthew 16:21–23. The Lord began to teach His disciples about His coming suffering and death. Peter evaluated what the Lord was saying, decided he didn't like it, took Him aside, and tried to straighten Him out.

Knowing that he had *some* of the right answers, Peter fell into the trap of thinking he had *all* the right answers—or at least *more* of the right answers than the Lord had at this point.

That's a glimpse of the inner-life-setting of Matthew 16:22. We are watching a man function with arrogant sincerity. Inaccurate self-talk will produce such a paradox. Matthew 16:23 contains Christ's rebuke to Peter. He put the disciple in Satan's camp. How did this make Peter feel? Did he have enough insight to work his way through such a stinging rebuke? Did the words in 16:24–28 speak to Peter's ego problems?

We could go on through the Gospels and study Peter's inner-life-setting in various situations—his vow never to disown the Lord, his threefold denial of Christ, his bitter weeping, his conversation with the risen Christ about loving sheep. Then we could turn to Acts, where Peter regains his boldness and loses his prejudice. And finally into his two letters where, among other things, he tells his readers to

> Humble yourselves, therefore, under God's mighty hand, that He may lift you up in due time (1 Peter 5:6).

Peter knew what he was talking about.

As we have said, some texts clearly present the inner-life-setting. Others do not. Where the text does do it, we should include it in our study and exposition. Where the inner-life-setting is not overtly stated, we should carefully probe the thoughts and feelings of the people involved and use these insights to enhance our communication of the truth. The Bible says too much about the inner man for us to neglect it in our preaching.[4] Developing the inner-life-setting will cause us to be more biographical in our study and our preaching of the biblical text. It will stimulate us to think personally as well as propositionally. It will enable us to develop not only the doctrine of the text, but also the drama of the text.

Whose inner life are we concerned about? Moses' inner life. Job's inner life. The psalmists' inner lives. Solomon's inner life. The prophets' inner lives. The disciples' inner lives. Luke's inner life. Paul's inner life. In short, the inner lives of all the biblical authors. What is going on inside these biblical authors as they wrote the inspired text is highly significant, because how they felt and thought influenced what they said and how they said it. It is up to the preacher to work diligently to understand both the text and what was going on in the life of the authors as they composed the text.

We are also to be concerned about the inner lives of the recipients of the text. What were they thinking and feeling as they read it or listened to someone else read it? Was this truth new to them? Reminding and reinforcing what they already knew? Correcting them? Convicting them? Complimenting them? Were they resisting? Accepting? The better we understand the inner life of the original recipients, the more relevant we can be to the inner life of the current recipients—namely, your congregation and you.

IN SUMMARY

The challenge of this chapter has been to creatively re-create the life-setting of the biblical text. "Life-setting" simply means the things that go on *in* and *around* and *between* the individual(s) associated with the text. The Scripture does not always reveal to us what these things are. To the extent that they would be helpful to our understanding and application of the text, we can legitimately use our imagination to creatively re-create certain significant aspects of the life-setting of that text. Our purpose is not to impose our culture and ideas on Scripture, but to expose interesting and informative details about the text—the obvious, and the not-so-obvious. Creativity and imagination are used to develop those things that are not immediately obvious.

We focused our attention on three selected facets of the life-setting of the text. First, we looked at different ways an author uses words to emphasize and intensify. Granted, it is all God's Word, but God does not communicate with an insipid monotone. We need to pay close attention to what He says and how He says it. Second, we devoted time to life-setting in its interpersonal dimension, showing how we can raise our antennae and fine-tune our receivers to pick up biblical conversations that will help us to understand and to apply the truths of the text. Third, we investigated inner-life-settings, directing our attention to what is or could be going on inside biblical characters. These people were not hollow servants. They were full of vim, vigor, and vitality, as well as some problems.

Life-settings are helpful. Use them!

4

Creatively Relating to the Life-Setting of the Congregation

We have been dealing with the life-setting of the text. Now it is time to move to the other side of the diagram and deal with the life-setting of the congregation.

TEXT	PREACHER PREACHING	CONGREGATION

Figure 4.1

Just as every text of Scripture has a life-setting, so every human being has a life-setting. Just as it is important for us to discover and develop the life-setting of the text, so it is also important for us to be aware of the life-setting of each member of the congregation. In this chapter we suggest a number of things that will help us become aware of and remain sensitive to the life-setting of the people to whom we minister.

CREATIVITY IN PREACHING

IDENTIFY YOUR PEOPLE: WHO ARE THEY?

Your congregation is more than a group of people who sit and listen to you preach every Sunday. Each person is unique, with numerous identities and multiple roles. Unless we keep these features in mind, we will easily revert to generalized preaching to a stereotyped audience.

"No," you say, "I offer my people a sermonic menu that has something for every individual; truth to meet every need." Perhaps you do now and then, but most of the time the menu stays in the study and all you offer is "Today's Special," which is usually designed for the white, middle-class, middle-aged, suburban male.

Who, then, are these customers who come your way each week to ingest your spiritual food? Well, for starters, they are *male and female*. Are you consciously, specifically speaking to both sexes in every sermon? Are you clearly and consistently serving the text to both men and women?

Let's keep going. You can identify your people as they relate to the area of marriage and family. Here is a suggested list:

children	mothers	separated
adopted	parents	fathers
divorced	childless	husbands
in-laws	remarried	relatives
wives	sisters	engaged
singles	grandparents	brothers
widowed		single parents

Every person in your congregation fits into a number of these categories. They are part of his or her life-setting. Every time you preach, single out one or more of these categories and relate the text to those needs.

Here is a list that moves into a number of other categories:

poor	young adult	sick
jogger	healthy	addicted

Creatively Relating to the Life-Setting of the Congregation

athlete	retired	failure
black	unemployed	successful
professional	pastor	minority
student	wealthy	dying
elderly	Hispanic	youth
disabled	career woman	deacon
self-employed		teacher

As you prepare for a coming sermon, let your mind roam through your congregation. The young people usually sit near the front on the left side. They are a fun-loving group of fellows and gals. Do you use humor now and then in your sermon? I hope so, because teenagers like to laugh, even in church.

Some of the teenagers are *athletes*. Is there some way you can tie the biblical text to winning and losing, playing first string or sitting on the bench, high scoring versus hardly ever scoring, submitting to the coach or "doing your own thing," losing your temper instead of keeping your cool, stewardship of our physical resources, acceptance of limitations?

Our four offspring were quite involved in junior high and high school sports. Audrey and I sought to integrate biblical principles with their athletic life-settings, hoping that our church would reinforce our messages to them. It didn't happen very often.

CONTEXTUALIZE YOUR PEOPLE: WHERE ARE THEY?

Your people live and work in a variety of environments. Life-setting preaching should prepare them to handle the problems and the opportunities wherever they find themselves. Here is a sampling of environmental factors to which we are exposed:

politics	pornography	leisure
taxes	newspapers	advertising
inflation	industry	motor homes

fitness	war	drugs
education	technology	movies
hijacking	magazines	economics
recreation	television	materialism
aerobics	nuclear power	prisons
business	humanism	nursing homes
unions	sex	job
money	feminism	vacations
radio	AIDS	computers
dating	medicine	art
science	death	birth
sports	credit	abortion
authority	pregnancy	crime
euthanasia	music	government
accidents	morality	terrorism
hospitals	prostitution	homosexuality
	space travel	

The list obviously could go on interminably. Every time we turn around, there is something new in our world to challenge us. Of what value is such a list to the preacher? Well, his assigned task is to equip people "to live self-controlled, upright and godly lives in this present age" (Titus 2:12). The list above is a good sampling of what the Christian has to face *now* in *this* present age. Illustrations can come from these areas. Applications can be made to these areas. Victories can be gained in these areas.

Now, with the sermon in mind that you are preparing for next Sunday, let your eyes roam up and down the three columns above. Do you see an area of obvious application? Do some of your people work in one of these fields? Has one of these topics been prominent in the news this week? Have you avoided one of these issues long enough?

Consider one category: *advertising*. Is there a clever, subtle ad the media is currently using to entice people—yes, even your people—to compromise their values? To spend money they don't have? To be more materialistic? Could this passage of Scripture alert them to the danger of compromise? Does it teach them how to be more discerning? Are there any other ways you could relate the truth of the text to the subtle deception of the ad?

What we are saying is that we need to teach people how to evaluate commercials on radio and TV, how to browse through newspapers and magazines, how to respond to half-price sales, how to handle coupons and rebates, because that's where people live—in an environment that is supersaturated with a materialistic system that is not heartily in favor of self-control and upright and godly living. You, the preacher, may be the only anti-materialistic voice they will hear crying in the wilderness of advertising, which ubiquitously surrounds them and subtly seeks to seduce them.

ANALYZE YOUR PEOPLE: WHAT ARE THEY THINKING? HOW ARE THEY FEELING?

The two preceding subjects tend to highlight the interpersonal aspects of life: who and where our people are, their roles and their relationships. Now we move inside and direct our attention to the *intra*personal—the inner-life-setting of the people in the congregation. Here are some of the mental and emotional options your people can bring to church with them.

interested	neutral	frustrated
proud	pessimistic	challenged
confused	rejoicing	apathetic
convicted	preoccupied	threatened
surprised	bored	motivated
peaceful	skeptical	afraid
optimistic	accepting	compassionate
excited	grieving	guilty
sobered	suspicious	rejected
inferior	worried	lonely
happy	tired	depressed
angry	antagonistic	tempted

Let's discuss a few of these emotions. Many people are *interested* in everything you say and in everything the church does; keep fanning their flame. Some are interested in gaining knowledge, but are not interested in making a commitment; along with the data you deliver, challenge them to a decision. A few are probably there under protest—perhaps a teenager, sitting in silent, sullen rebellion against her parents who made her come, or an unsaved spouse whose mate cajoled him into attending. In either case, your task is to say and do things that will stimulate interest in God and the gospel.

Some are *confused*. They don't clearly understand what it takes to be a Christian, or they have been talking with a member of a cult who lives next door. They need clear, specific truths related to their personal dilemmas. Furthermore, they need to know it is not wrong to be confused; it is wrong to *stay* confused.

A few are *grieving*. Bill's fiancée just broke their engagement. Sally's mother has cancer. Wendell got laid off. Martha failed her driver's license exam. Show yourself sensitive to these kinds of situations and people will not only come to hear you preach, they will sit near the front!

Happiness is the possession of some. The kids have recovered from the chicken pox, Charlie got a raise, Pam got a date, Hal got a ten-speed bike—and they are all in the Sunday morning service, each so excited that they have trouble concentrating on your sermon. You have to make them believe that what you have to say is more important and more exciting than anything else in all this world, *and/or* you have to relate their happiness to God and His Word.

These are not only words that describe where people are; they are words that indicate where people can and should be. The person who comes to church feeling rejected should leave feeling accepted. The envious should go away with a new level of contentment. The bored should be challenged. And because there are things in life that may always be boring (such as pulling weeds or sweeping floors), the bored should learn to cope with boredom. Let it not be a boring sermon with which they have to cope!

These are not only words that describe the congregation; they might well describe the preacher. Ideally, the man in the pulpit should be peaceful, motivated, confident, accepted, and optimistic. Realistically, he may on occasion be confused, threatened, worried, and tired. This is where openness can be powerful, for this is where the transparent preacher can function, in Henri Nouwen's words, as "the wounded healer."[1] It takes one to know one, and to be one.

No one comes to church void of all thoughts and feelings. Everyone brings certain pieces of mental and emotional baggage to the preaching service. We would like for the people to check their bags at the door and come in empty, ready and willing to be filled. If that doesn't happen, we would like to have security checkpoints in the narthex, and as each one went through the scanner, we would get a computer screen readout of the mental and emotional state of every individual. Instead, in they come, bags and all, and it then becomes the awesome responsibility of the preacher to help people unlock, unzip, unpack, evaluate, and throw away or keep, repack, zip, and lock. You may want to "bag" this whole illustration, but it is one way to picture the process of preaching. If, during the week, a lot of suit(able) case searching is going on in the life of the preacher and the people, things will open up better on Sunday.

WHAT TO DO WITH LIFE-SETTING DATA

We have developed three extensive lists. The first identifies the people: who they are. The second contextualizes the people: where they are. The third analyzes the people: what they are thinking and feeling. How can we use this data? Type it all on one page, putting the appropriate word lists under each heading. Keep this sheet someplace in your study where it is always handy for you to look at— preferably where it is staring you right in the face. As you prepare your messages, periodically gaze at this list, asking yourself how you can relate this truth to in-laws, retired persons, a coming election, and so on.

As I gaze through the words on these lines, I think

about my sermon *introduction*. Perhaps there is some *antagonism* on the part of youth. Then I might start out with: "It is quite possible that some of you may not agree with what I have to say this morning . . . so I ask all of you to please listen carefully to the sermon. . . ." Or, "You've had a good week . . . things went well at home and on the job . . . in a word, you were *successful*. Why? Why did you succeed? What did you do that made you successful? Is there something basic and foundational to success? The Word of God provides insight into the answer to these questions. Open your Bibles to . . ." Introductions can easily and often be drawn from the life-settings of the people in your church. Glancing through these lists will provide the stimulus you need to develop meaningful and varied introductions.

You can also use these life-setting lists to prompt *illustrations*. For example, every person falls into one of three categories—children, youth, or adults—and, to a greater or lesser extent, they are all aware of the other two categories besides their own. So illustrations from the experiences of adults, youth, and children ought to be developed and used frequently, because when you do this you get on the wavelength of every person in your congregation. But remember, we said earlier that our bias is toward white, middle-aged, middle-income, suburban males. To balance that, I strongly suggest that you also use plenty of illustrations from and for the lives of children, youth, and women. Adults will always listen to what you say to and about their children and young people. The reverse is not true.

Contextualize your illustrations. If your youth are dating, illustrate from boy-girl relationships. If some of your men travel, illustrate from the tempting magazines in the airport shops. In the summer, illustrate from vacations. Dealing with cheating? Illustrate just before final exams are given. Do you see my point? The environmental list is replete with sermon illustration potential. So is the thought/feeling list. You can illustrate with stories of sorrow, anger, happiness, and everything in between. That's where people live. Enrich the text and enlighten your congregation with life-centered illustrations.

HOW TO SECURE THIS LIFE-SETTING DATA

How do we get this kind of biographical information about people that will continually apprise us as to who they are, where they are, what they are thinking, how they are feeling? Here are some ways that work for me. Try them on and see how they fit you.

1. Visit your people in their homes, schools, jobs, and leisure pursuits. The church is your turf. Those other places constitute their turf. Meet them there. Talk with them there. This is their world. Know where they live, where they work, where they go to school, what their hobbies are. Find out what is involved in the life of Ben, Carla, and the rest.

2. Ask questions. Good preachers know how to ask questions and listen to the answers. Learn from them and about them. Ernest Hemingway said, "I have never spent an hour with a man that I couldn't write his biography." Develop this kind of an insatiable appetite for information about people.

3. Read. You can learn much about the world in which your people live by reading books and magazines. *Business Week, Sports Illustrated, Psychology Today, Reader's Digest* will provide all kinds of insights for relevant introductions, illustrations, and applications. Dip into best sellers, both fiction and nonfiction; find out why they are so popular. I know—you can't afford all this reading material. So use the public library. Find out who reads in your congregation, and borrow from them. I know—you don't have time to read. Make time. I know—you're a slow reader. Take a rapid reading course. I know—you read the newspaper, *Leadership, Christianity Today*, and *Moody Monthly*. Broaden your horizons.

4. Listen to National Public Radio. Watch educational television. Both these organizations do some fine reporting journalism, most of the time in greater depth than regular

radio and TV stations. *All Things Considered* is a late afternoon program of NPR that provides excellent exposure to a broad range of news. Without commercials.

5. Consider service clubs: Rotary, Kiwanis, the Lions, and so on. If you join, you have to get involved through both regular attendance and active service. Weekly programs expose you to what's going on in your community. If you don't choose to join, ask others who are members to take you now and then.

6. Take advantage of opportunities provided by local colleges and universities. Continuing education courses are always available. They will enrich your own life and your ministry. Special lectures are often held in different colleges, different departments. Encourage college students in your church to let you know when special programs are scheduled.

7. Attend professional seminars. I almost hesitate to mention these, since we are seminar saturated to the point that local church ministry is something we do between seminars. But there are many good ones. Consider inviting some of your lay leaders to attend ministry seminars with you. It will help to equip them, and it will help them better understand what you do. Then turn that around and ask them on occasion to take you to one of their professional meetings or seminars. It may help to sharpen some of your own skills, introduce you to new subjects and ideas, and increase your understanding of the life-setting of some members of your congregation.

8. Form a sermon preparation and evaluation team. This is one of the most productive things I have ever done in my pastoral ministry. Form a team that is representative of your congregation—male, female, young, old, thinker, doer, traditional, contemporary, and so on. Six to ten people would be a good number. Ask them to meet with you for an hour and half in the middle of the week for a period of one to three months.

THE PREPARATION AND EVALUATION TEAM

There are two items on the agenda at a midweek sermon preparation and evaluation meeting as suggested above. First, an evaluation of last Sunday's message. Second, preparation of next Sunday's message. Evaluation doesn't come easy. Laypeople are not used to doing it, are often not trained to do it, and in some instances don't think it should be done: the Lord's anointed are not to be touched! But with an openness on the part of the rest of the team, it can become a very profitable session, with plenty of positive as well as some negative feedback.

Help in preparation goes like this: The pastor shares the passage he will be using, gives them the general outline he will follow, and the overall thrust he expects the message to have. The team members point out where they need a clearer understanding of the text; how they see the truth applying to their lives and the lives of their children, their friends; ways in which the truth could be illustrated; and what should be emphasized. The results: a pastor who starts preparing earlier, a group of laypeople who become more intelligently involved in *helping* the pastor develop his sermon, who *listen* intently on Sunday morning to see how he *and they* are doing, and who evaluate both strengths and weaknesses in order to help their pastor grow.

At times I have gone through this process with adult and youth Sunday school teachers and tied the sermon and Sunday school lesson together. On occasion I have met immediately after the morning service with the team for an evaluation while things were fresh in their minds. I have used the entire midweek prayer and study group as a preparation and evaluation team. You could use members of your staff, members of your board, interns, or Bible college and seminary students to team up with you in this kind of endeavor. It will make you a better preacher, not only because you are asking for and receiving evaluation, but also because you are preparing your sermons *with* people as well as *for* people.[2]

IN SUMMARY

Nobody "just preaches the Word." When you preach, you always preach the Word *to people*. The crucial question is, how well do you know people? This chapter has been designed to remind you of various ways you can determine and use the current life-settings of the people. Remaining ever-sensitive to who they are, where they are, what they are thinking, and how they are feeling will allow us to scratch where they itch.

5

Creatively Using the Life-Setting of the Preacher

In the preceding chapters we have dealt with the life-setting of the ancient biblical text and the life-setting of the present-day congregation. Who links the text and the congregation together? The preacher. How does he do it? *With his own life-setting.* He has one, you know. Just because he is on his way to heaven doesn't mean he has checked out of this world. Upon graduating from Bible college or seminary, he didn't have to turn in his humanity to receive his diploma. Every preacher brings to the task of preaching his own personal, unique life-setting. We need to explore this concept.

YOUR PERSONAL ENDOWMENTS

Your sex, size, shape, strength, coordination, face, voice—in short, all of your physical endowments—make you a human being similar to all others. Yet experience proves that nobody looks, walks, or talks exactly like you. You are a unique person, recognizably distinct from all other humans. Furthermore, like others, you have a mind, emotions, and will. But you don't think, feel, and act exactly like anyone else, so once again you must regard yourself as unique, with a personality that is recognizably distinct from everyone else. Finally, you have certain gifts and talents that make it possible for you to do certain things exceedingly well. Other human beings also have skills, even some of the same ones you have, but each person packages and delivers these skills in and through unique individualities. You are a custom-made person.

Custom-made by whom? Ultimately, by God. "It is he who made us," said the psalmist (100:3). David personalizes and localizes God's creative handiwork: "For you created my inmost being; you knit me together in my mother's womb. . . . I am fearfully and wonderfully made; your works are wonderful, I know that full well" (139:13–14). Isaiah comes to the same conclusion: "We are the clay, you are the potter; we are all the work of your hand" (64:8). To any dissatisfied with the divine design in us, Isaiah issues a solemn warning: "Woe to him who quarrels with his Maker" (45:9). The clay does not talk back to the Potter.

Moses expands our concept of customizing with the revelation that God gave the Israelite craftsmen all the skills needed to build the tabernacle (Exod. 31:1–6). And of course, the gifts of the Spirit, which all believers possess, are not the result of our choice or of mere chance. The Holy Spirit "gives them to each one, just as he determines" (1 Cor. 12:11).

Your physical being, the components of your personality, your talents and gifts all combine to make you a unique person. Behind your uniqueness is a sovereign, creative God. He has an infinite number of patterns to choose from. When He made you, He chose one He had never used before; when He finished you, He retired the pattern. There never has been one exactly like you. There will never be another exactly like you. You are one of a kind.[1]

YOUR RESPONSE TO YOUR ENDOWMENTS

Get in close touch with your God-ordained uniqueness. Discover and develop your God-given strengths. Identify and accept your God-allowed limitations. Find out who you are physically, mentally, emotionally, and volitionally. Determine what you can do with your talents and gifts. As you discover and develop your uniqueness as a *person*, realize that you are also discovering and developing your uniqueness as a *preacher*. There is only one person like you. Thus there is only one preacher like you. Your obligation is to find out who you are and then *be* yourself to the full, with excellence.

You will discover things about yourself that you wish were different. Some you can change, some you can't. You may wish you were taller, but you aren't and never will be. Accept yourself at 5'6'' and lower the pulpit or stand on a stool. You long for a mellifluous bass voice, but your vocal cords operate to deliver a high-pitched, slightly raspy tone. Voice lessons may help, but you will probably have to settle for something less than bass, unless you can live with a low-level cold for the rest of your ministry! You wish you could probe deeper in your study of the Word, but you're just not as analytic as others you know. However, you delight in synthesizing—that is, putting ideas together so they form an understandable whole. God has fashioned you as He wanted you to be fashioned. Don't quarrel with your Maker. Cooperate with Him.

Many things can be changed. Your teeth are crooked? An orthodontist can help. Have a shoulder slump? Stand up straight. You lisp? See a speech therapist. Have a facial tic or body twitch? Consult a physician or psychologist. A mole on your chin? Try a dermatologist. Tend to be soft-spoken? Learn to project your voice, and turn up the volume on the PA system. Carrying too much weight? Eat less and exercise more. Color blind? Have your wife choose your ties. Put your hand in your pocket when you preach? Sew the pocket shut. Too many "you knows" and "uhs"? Listen to yourself on tape. Have someone count them for you. Expunge the majority of these "filler" words from your speaking. You know, you don't have to say them, you know. Uh . . . ya know whatta mean?

Even when you change many of these kinds of idiosyncrasies, you will still be the unique you. This unique you is one major part of your life-setting. What you have been endowed with, you preach with. Watch out for the copy-cat mentality that pressures you to be like someone else. The other guy appears to be popular and successful, and he well may be, but there is only one person in all this world exactly like him—that's he. You can't be his clone. Don't try to be. Be your God-ordained self. Your inherent, intrinsic characteristics and qualities are what make you you. Stay consistently and clearly in touch with who you are and what you can and can't do. In other words, discover your own personal equation: **John Jones = a + b + c - d.** Your life-setting is not just *where* you are, it is also *who* you are, and who you are will significantly influence *how* you prepare and preach.

YOUR PERSONAL EXPERIENCES

Your personal endowments are the inherent characteristics, qualities, and aptitudes that God has bestowed on you. Your personal experiences are the events that happen in your life. We know that all these events are a part of God's sovereign plan for us. What we may classify as good and bad ultimately all work together for our good (Rom. 8:28). Solomon listed twenty-eight different human experiences, fourteen of them positive, fourteen of them negative, at least from our standpoint. Yet from his inspired perspective he went on to classify all twenty-eight of them as "beautiful" (Eccl. 3:1–11).

Paul speaks to the same concept when he declares that God "works out everything in conformity with the purpose of his will" (Eph. 1:11). Each and every experience in life is a part of God's purpose and plan. It is for your learning and His glory. All these divinely arranged experiences constitute your life-setting, from birth to death. The "you" that preaches is the "you" that was born, raised, fed, clothed, spanked, educated, hurt, employed, married, misunderstood, honored—and all the myriad other experiences that make you an authentic member of the human race. All the experiences you have had and will have are potential bridges linking the text to the congregation and the congregation to the text. Let's explore this bridging operation.

YOUR USE OF YOUR EXPERIENCES

1. Remembering Your Past

Two things you can be sure of. You had many, many experiences while you were growing up that are common to everyone else. At the same time, you had some experiences unique to you. All these experiences can be used to enhance your preaching. One of the basic problems is that you have forgotten much of these data. They are piled up in the various storerooms of your mind, and many of the doors are shut, some even locked. What to do? Start writing your autobiography. Not a formal, fancy treatment of your life, but a listing of the various things that you remember happening along the way. Keep this list handy, and every time you think of another experience, write it down. Here are some things from my list (most I remember, some my parents told me about):

Born in Prescott, the mile-high city of Arizona
Hospital I was born in burned down shortly thereafter
Remember going down steep, snow-covered hill on sled in winter
Big bonfires at top and bottom of sledding hill
Played under the ironing board and it collapsed on me
Fell out of our moving car when I was four—not hurt badly
Used to watch Dad shovel coal into the basement furnace
Stuffed leaves way up both nostrils—had to go to the doctor

Played with Tommy who lived next door
Had difficulty learning to ride bike, kept running
into the wall
Rode a school bus to kindergarten
Hit a kid over the head with my chocolate milk bottle
on the school bus
Some older kids pushed me into a trench and
wouldn't let me out till supper
Fell out of bed and hurt my back on my mucilage
bottle
Had one sister, three years younger than I
Got sick and had to come home and take a nap every
day in third grade
Shattered my parents' bedroom window with my BB
gun
Had a crush on Prina Stanley in fourth grade
Member of a gang that harassed kids who weren't for
Franklin D. Roosevelt in fifth grade

These incidents are a mere beginning. I use these kinds
of personal vignettes primarily for illustrations and applications. These childhood life-settings will capture the attention
of every person in your congregation, young and old.

What I am suggesting is that you develop a similar list
of your own childhood experiences—a list that you can look
at as you prepare your sermons, and a list that you can add
to along the way as other events come to mind. Just as God
has uniquely endowed each of us, so He has given each of us
a unique set of growing-up experiences.

Next move into your teenage years. Record some of the
experiences you had at home with parents, brothers and
sisters, other relatives, and friends. List all the different
places you went on family vacations. Jot down the names of
the teachers you remember, the subjects you took, the teams
you played on, the embarrassing moments you agonized
through, highlights of your boy-girl relationships, hilarious
things that happened to you, ways and means you were
disciplined, honors and awards you received, whether you
were an introvert or an extrovert, a leader or a follower,

intelligent or not so, all the hobbies you had, gregarious or a loner, shy or outgoing. In other words, begin to remember and write down some of the specific, intensely personal details of your youth.

Here is a category you won't want to leave out: all the jobs you had while you were growing up. Here's my list:

washed windows	picked cotton	worked on ranch
stock clerk	trained horses	cleaned test tubes
picked acorns	swept floors	cleaned stables
drove a tractor	sales clerk	built fences
mowed lawns	baling hay	delivery boy
milked cows	night irrigator	drove a truck
camp counselor	dynamite blasting	worked for veterinarian

A wealth of illustrations and applications is bound up in all these part-time jobs. They will help you recognize how varied your experience is, and it will alert your listeners to the fact that you have done something besides preach.

Naturally you would want to trace your spiritual pilgrimage through your childhood and teenage years. Did you grow up in a Christian home? Was church a vital part of your earlier years? Did you run around with Christian friends? When did you become a Christian? Did you pray? Read your Bible? Did you ever get in big trouble? Did you attend Christian or public schools? Did you use profanity? Drugs? Tobacco? Alcohol? What kind of sexual temptations did you struggle with? What people were positive/negative role models for you? Were you rebellious? Did you ever run away from home? Did you ever want to? What kinds of things dominated your life—sports, job, girlfriend or boyfriend, cars, music, hobbies?

I stress writing these things down, because you won't remember all of them when you are putting a sermon together. If you have a list, you can quickly peruse it and pick out something that ties right in with your message.

A word to those who want to forget their past,

especially when it contains a lot of gross sin: You would rather not think about it or talk about it. You would like to bury it once and for all. In the words of Paul, you would like to forget the past and focus on the future (Phil. 3:12–14). Certainly that is a worthy goal, but remember also that God allowed you to have those varied experiences in your background and may want to use you to warn others. Insights from your experience can be powerful persuaders to help young people avoid those sins or extract themselves from them. You need not parade your past in front of people, but you should not hide it either.

I also find that uniquely talented people who get saved often want to walk away from their field of expertise because they used it in a secular, non-Christian context. For instance, the brilliant trumpet player who meets Christ and decides to go into the ministry. His trumpet becomes a symbol of his pre-salvation days—with all their sin and self-centeredness—and thus he wants to put it away and close that chapter of his life. As a result, a lot of talent will not be used for the glory of the God who bestowed it.

2. Revealing Your Present

We have been urging you to dig into your past and use it in your preaching. It will do wonders to help you authenticate your humanity and validate your credibility. It is a natural way of using your past life-setting to creatively communicate truth to people. Another important dimension of your life-setting is your immediate present, that is, what is happening now in your life.

It is easier to capture and record our present experience than it is to remember our past. Past experiences have a way of slipping away from us. However, it is probably harder to reveal to others what is happening right now in our lives than it is to tell what happened way back when. Yet everybody else has a present life-setting with which they are having to deal. Why not us? What is happening now in your *marriage?* What new things are you learning about marriage in general, your partner and you in particular? When do you find time in your busy schedules to talk? What is fairly easy to talk about, and what is more difficult? What are your differences? Are you currently working on any goals in your marriage? Do you make yourselves accountable to each other with regard to these goals? Any accountability to a third party, another couple, a small group, or the entire congregation? What creates problems in your marriage? What helps to solve the problems?

If you seldom or never say anything from the pulpit about your marriage, what messages may you be conveying? That it is not important. That it is none of their business. That everything is just great. That there are problems, but you won't say anything about them. That the whole subject is too intimate to be discussed publicly. This last statement is probably the clincher. We struggle with how to deal with intimate issues in our preaching and usually opt for silence or superficiality. If we do decide to deal with the intimate issues, we still tend to say little or nothing about ourselves in relation to the issue.

If you are married, you have a marital life-setting just as all the married couples in your congregation do. The only way you can really connect with them is to mention your marriage as well as theirs. Do it discreetly and with dignity. Do it openly and honestly, yet sensitively and appropriately. Do it not to embarrass, but to edify. Keep it in balance. Present the positive (changes, progress, victories) as well as the negative (struggles, frustrations, failures).

What is happening now in your *family*? How old are your children? How are they different from each other and from their parents? How are they similar to Mom and Dad? How do they like school, church, sports, or music? Do they fight? Whine? Resist? Forget? Rebel? Sulk? Scream? Everybody else's kids do, how come yours don't? Oh, they do, you say. Well, how come you never mention it from the pulpit? Because down in the inner recesses of your being there is a little voice called "ego" and whenever you are tempted to admit that your offspring are normal, at times subnormal, your ego whispers, "Don't tell 'em, preacher; they desperately need someone to look up to, and for such a time as this, you're the man." The mask is put in place.

What about your parental behavior in the home? Are you consistent in establishing and enforcing the rules? Are you and your wife a parenting team? Does Mom do the threatening while Dad does the thrashing? Are you so caught up in trying to counteract your own family background that you have swung past the midpoint and gone to the other extreme? Would you dare breathe a word of this to your congregation, or are you letting the ego convince you that you should keep quiet about your family affairs until you have your parenting act together. Then you will tell all. The mask remains in place—to the detriment of everyone.

What is happening in *you*? Plenty. All week long you have been busy in the ministry. Busy studying. Busy writing. Busy talking. Busy listening. Busy praying. Busy helping. Busy counseling. You have had to cope with failure, frustration, a bit of depression, some anger, criticism, and inadequacies. At the same time you have helped three people come to know Christ as their Lord and Savior. The monthly board meeting went smoothly. Congregational giving is up. Your sermon outline jelled on Tuesday. That note of appreciation came in the mail on Thursday. Now it is Sunday morning. In a few moments you will step to the pulpit and preach. You have done your homework—you know *what* you are going to preach. You have been with your people—you know *to whom* you are going to preach. Your text is 1 Corinthians 12:25–26:

> . . . so that there should be no division in the body, but that its parts should have equal concern for each other. If one part suffers, every part suffers with it; if one part is honored, every part rejoices with it.

In your sermon you point out that this text is using the human body to illustrate how the spiritual body, the church, should function. People in the church should have mutual concern for each other. That is the principle in verse 25.

Two specific implications or illustrations are given in verse 26. If a member of the church is suffering, all the other members of the church should suffer with that one, and if a member is honored, all the other members should rejoice with that one. That is the way a healthy human body functions. If there is pleasure in the taste buds, the whole body licks its lips. That's assuming there is a healthy communication system operating in the human body. The same ought to be true in the church. If there are open, honest relationships in the local church, then no one suffers alone and no one rejoices alone.

At this point you relate this truth to the life-setting of your congregation by mentioning the fact that Fred Martin got laid off from his job last week and their third baby is due in a month. The Martins are hurting—and the entire body is going to help them bear the burden. You also announce that Jody Bird and Chet Jordan have just become engaged and will be married soon. The informed body rejoices with Jody and Chet. In the coming weeks, many members will be involved in helping this young couple prepare for the wedding and married life.

Now comes a crucial moment in your sermon. You have struggled all week with the idea of sharing something from your own life-setting—a matter of suffering, a matter of rejoicing. Your internal dialogue has gone like this:

"The truths of this passage apply to all members of the body, pastors included."

"I know that, but at the same time I am to be one they look up to, a leader who is more than a conqueror, one who should be mastering the problems of life on a day-to-day basis."

"Okay, then tell them all about these daily victories."

"Well, as a matter of fact, I have a day of defeat now and then."

"Tell them about that too."

"I'm afraid they will lose confidence in me if I share a personal problem from the pulpit."

"And I'm afraid that I'll come across as boasting, if I share an area of success."

"So you want to be one of those middle-of-the-road ministers—nice, neat, and neutral, a cool dude who conveys to everyone that you've got your act together."

"No, I would really like to be appropriately honest about some of the positives and negatives in my life, but frankly, I'm afraid to try it."

But you did! You mentioned that you constantly struggle with the problem of doing things at the last moment, and asked your people to pray for you and hold you accountable. Then you took a few moments and detailed a couple of things you did last week to build your relationship with your wife and children. As a result of these two unveilings, your credibility as a person, pastor, and preacher is on the rise.[2]

3. Projecting Into the Future

We have talked about remembering your past and revealing your present. Doing these allows you to creatively use your life-setting in your preaching. There is one more dimension to your life-setting that needs attention. It is the future.

We all like to think and plan ahead. We look forward to Thanksgiving, then Christmas, then New Year's, then spring break, then summer vacation. We anticipate events such as birthdays, anniversaries, graduation, buying a new car, taking a trip, adding a room to the house, adding a baby to the family, and so on. Though earthbound and time-constrained, we have been given the ability by God to think beyond the here, beyond the now. So we dream dreams and set goals—for tomorrow, next week, next month, next year. We project ourselves, our ministries, our churches, into the future. Why?

Because the just are to live by faith, and faith has to do with what we hope for, yet what we do not see (Heb. 11:1). If you have the gift of faith, then you are endowed with the unique, God-given ability to envision what needs to be done; what can be done. God has bestowed on you the capacity to combine insight and foresight. You have the virtues of a fanatic, without the vices. Such a gift tends to make you a futurist. A significant aspect of your life-setting is prophetic. As you link the text of Scripture to the congregation, you are not doing it just to inform them, but also to motivate and mobilize them with reference to what God can and will do in the future—the future of their church and their lives.

Even if you don't possess the gift of faith, you are still obligated to be competent in believing, for without faith it is impossible to please God (Heb. 11:6; cf. Matt. 6:30; Gal. 3:11; Col. 2:6–7). Thus, any and all preachers should be persons of faith, persons who are constantly extending their life-setting into the future. So let your people in on what you see God doing in your life and theirs in the coming days. What character qualities do you want to develop? What weaknesses do you want to strengthen? What skills do you want to sharpen and refine? What habits of holiness do you want to inculcate?

In what direction do you see the church going? What new programs do you see needed? What staff needs are you projecting? Where do you want to plant a new church? What target groups should be evangelized? What numerical growth are you aiming for? It won't all be positive. Faith sees what God can do in us and through us. Faith also sees what can happen if we remain ignorant or continue to disobey God. The preacher must warn as well as command and challenge. He must share his burdens and fears as well as his aspirations.

It's risky to dream out loud. You will receive criticism

and rejection. There may be nonchalance and apathy that will slowly deflate your ego and enthusiasm. There can be premature commitment, where people jump on your bandwagon for a while and then slide off when the road gets rough and you aren't looking. Share your burdens and your visions. Introduce them slowly. Explain them carefully. Be persistent without being obnoxious. Be patient without getting depressed. Try out the radical ideas first on your board, your staff, and other opinion leaders in your congregation. Inevitably you will find other visionaries in your church. They may be on your wavelength or on one of their own. So you will have to listen as well as talk. You will have to be open to their suggestions, as you expect them to be open to yours. Preachers do not have a monopoly on new ideas.

We repeat, it is risky to dream out loud. It is threatening to pry the lid off your fantasies and dreams and then pour them out in public where people can listen to them, analyze them, evaluate them, and accept or reject them. We all have a fear of intimacy. Even the congregation is a bit uneasy when the preacher bares his soul, because that forces each listener to grapple with his or her goals for the future— goals that may be diametrically different from the preacher's, or goals that may be nonexistent.

A well-rounded life-setting can and should include one's thoughts and feelings about the future. It is a tragedy for the preacher to omit these factors from his sermons. It only serves to dilute his message by deleting a critical dimension from the act of preaching.

IN SUMMARY

We have highlighted the sovereignty of God as it relates to your personal endowments and your personal experiences. We then underscored the importance of appropriate self-disclosure, whereby your sermons can be creatively enhanced by remembering your past, revealing your present, and projecting your future. The goal of the chapter is to make you more human, more transparent, more competent, and more aware of your uniqueness as a preacher. Now it is up to you. Make up the suggested lists and use them regularly.

6

Creative Audio and Print Media in Preaching

Question: If the Holy Spirit were to write a book on creative preaching, how many pages would it have?

Answer: It would have an infinite number of pages.

That's a lot of pages. But the fact that the Holy Spirit is omniscient demands the answer stated above. There are an infinite number of ways He can communicate truth. The fact that every human being is a uniquely endowed and uniquely experienced individual also supports the answer. There are an infinite number of ways the Holy Spirit can communicate truth *through us*. Though we all preach the same Word, and though we are all indwelt by the same Spirit, nobody preaches exactly like anyone else.

No, we are not going to try to stuff infinity into the next two chapters. Rather, we are going to continue to expand our homiletical horizons to allow us to see more options and alternatives in our preaching. We have defined creativity as the ability to take the things that have been created and use them in new and different ways. The text of Scripture has been brought into being by God. We don't create the text. We seek to understand it and communicate it creatively, that is, in new and different ways.

CREATIVITY IN PREACHING

It would be presumptuous of me to intimate that everything I present is new and different and that my ideas are comprehensive and complete. I am in process, just as you are. Some of my ideas will be familiar. Let them be an encouraging reinforcement to your ministry. Some will be new. Let them be a challenge to you. Be slow to reject them. Be willing to try them. Adapt them to your God-given uniqueness.

When we explore creative ways of communicating truth, we have to be careful not to allow the method to dominate the message. We have an unbridled commitment to study the Word carefully and to preach it consistently. A selected assortment of different ways to do this is not to prompt preachers to be clever, cute or weird. It is to stimulate them to realize that there is more than one best way to preach; as a matter of fact, there are more than a few good ways to preach. For each of us, there are an unlimited number of good ways to preach. We aren't trying to foment fads; we are earnestly seeking to facilitate the transfer of ideas and the transformation of individuals.

A WORD ABOUT VARIETY

Variety not only keeps us on the Holy Spirit's track, but also facilitates an effective *redundancy*. People need reminders and review to reinforce what they know (2 Peter 1:12–15). When we say the same things over and over, we are being redundant. There is a purposeful redundancy, designed to reduce uncertainty. However, if we repeat things over and over in essentially the same way, we are being boringly repetitious—I say, boringly repetitious. Hear me now, I mean boringly repetitious. Vary the ways you communicate the same truth, and you will have a more effective redundancy.

If we use the same techniques over and over, eventually our preaching will become too *predictable*. High predictability can lessen listener attention and concentration. It can have a numbing, neutralizing effect on those members of the congregation who are still awake. Variety will produce a measure of anticipation that will attract and hold the listeners' attention. But don't push a good thing too far. To be totally unpredictable in your preaching methodology is too unsettling for people. We all need a certain amount of routine.

Variety facilitates our ability to relate to individual members of the congregation. People listen, learn, and respond in different ways and at different rates. We vary our preaching methods to take these individual differences into account. Furthermore, if we use a variety of preaching methods and employ them effectively, we provide a powerful, positive model for the preaching and teaching staff and for the young men and women in the congregation who will one day be in the ministry.

That is how the theory works. Now let's turn to specific practice.

USING THE TAPE RECORDER

The first and most important use of the tape recorder is to record our sermons and listen to them. Do it at least once a month for the first three years of your ministry; two or three times a year after that. The tape recorder does not lie.

Put Scripture readings on tape for a change of pace in the morning worship service. Use someone who has a good voice and knows how to do interpretive reading.[1] Put a cross reference on tape instead of having everybody look it up and then reading it to them. Suppose you are preaching on the nature of the human heart from Mark 7:17–23. You might pause for a moment and say:

> "The prophet Jeremiah also understood the nature of the human heart, and spoke clearly about it. Listen carefully to what he had to say."

On tape, and probably best when put through your sound system, booms the voice of Jeremiah, slowly and deliberately saying:

"The heart is deceitful above all things and beyond cure" (Jeremiah 17:9).

Jeremiah might repeat it for emphasis or add verse 10. Suppose there is an interpretation of the text totally different from yours. You want to mention it and deal with it. Why not put it on tape and run it through your sound system at the appropriate time in the sermon? Or you talked with someone during the week who has been struggling with the problem on which you are preaching. Capture in capsule form your conversation on tape.

You might put some live opinion interviews on tape. Approach people in the shopping mall, or in the church parking lot, and ask them what they think about capital punishment, nuclear war, Christians running for president, God, the church—whatever it is you are preaching about. Put germane comments through the sound system. They will add a fresh breath of secular reality to your sermon.

The inner struggles of one's conscience in the heat of temptation can be recorded and played. Even possible attitudes or questions that members of the congregation might have about the message could be put on tape. At the beginning of the sermon you say:

"I'm preaching on prophecy this morning. I wish I could read some of your minds. I'd sure like to know . . . honestly now . . . what you really think about prophecy . . ."

And on tape comes a number of individuals candidly voicing their opinions:

"Prophecy scares me to death. If I wasn't sitting up near the front, I'd leave right now."

"It's all about the future . . . way up in heaven. Why don't you talk about something practical . . . for me . . . right here and now."

"Oh boy, another eschatological escapade . . . telling us which prophetic prefix we hold to . . . pre-, post-, mid-, or a-! I'm confused! Why didn't God give us a simple timetable that everybody can agree on."

There are some useful guidelines for using a tape recorder in worship. Use good equipment—tapes, recorders, and PA. Don't talk too fast. Rehearse until it becomes natural. A script will save you lots of time. Avoid last-minute preparation; you will seldom get quality under pressure. Keep it short; one or two minutes is plenty. Don't use *your* voice on tape, unless it's your conscience or your struggles; use the voices of people in the congregation. Look for those with skills in reading, interpreting, and acting. Use men's and women's voices. Use children, youth, and adults.

USING LIVE VOICES

Everything we have just mentioned with regard to the tape recorder can also be done live, with the person visible in the congregation or unseen offstage. The main point of this is to move away from monologue for a moment and engage in dialogue. Because it is different, and thus relatively unpredictable, it will always capture the immediate, total attention of each person in the congregation. You might plan to have someone interrupt you at a prearranged point to challenge a concept you are developing, or to ask a question prompted by your message, or to seek clarification.

Suppose you are preaching on 2 Timothy 2:22 and are developing the first clause: "Flee the evil desires of youth." A teenager's voice might come into the room from an offstage mike, saying:

"My friends and I need a bit of help. Every time we hear this from you adults, it seems to end up as a reference to sex. We are beginning to get the impression that life for us teenagers is basically staying away from each other."

Now you have everyone's undivided attention. You can go ahead and dialogue with the offstage teenager, letting the congregation listen in on your conversation, or you can inform the congregation that the question is valid and you intend to address it.

When you use this method, realize that you are attempting to raise and deal with the kinds of questions that members of your congregation are or should be asking. On occasion you or another person can play the devil's advocate. Or one person can represent the entire congregation and become its alter ego.

One Sunday evening I was preaching on the authority of Scripture. There were many college students in the congregation, some of whom I knew were struggling with believing in the authority of a text written thousands of years ago; skeptical about inspiration, inerrancy, and so on. So I worked with a layman during the week; then, while I was preaching, he would pose, at prearranged points in a slightly skeptical way, the kinds of questions the collegians were asking or were being asked by their skeptical, unsaved peers. We answered the questions from the text. Dialogue of this sort need not eliminate exposition.

The person can dialogue with you in the sanctuary— from the platform, from the choir, from the balcony, from the main floor. Someone might ask for, or give, an illustration or application of the truth you are presenting. One could heartily agree with an idea you are presenting. If you are presenting something that is a bit different from the traditional approach—say, for example, a contextual interpretation of Revelation 3:20—you will have some uneasy, startled people. Why not hear from one or two of them?

Some guidelines for planned dialogue are appropriate. A good sound system helps. Also be aware of the potential shock to the audience when a voice cries out of the wilderness! Your response should be somewhere between surprise and nonchalance. Resist the temptation to overstate your case or overwhelm the other person in the dialogue. Relate your comments to the biblical text. You can have the person spontaneously interrupt you, or you can request the response. If you do the latter, make sure your planned partner speaks out quickly; somebody else may want to get into the act without a script! Natural humor arises easily out of these dialogues; just don't let it get out of hand. Practice.

Practice on location. Quit while you are ahead; allow two to three minutes at the most for this exercise.

INTERVIEWING INDIVIDUALS

Tuesday noon you have lunch with Dan Wright. He shares with you how he is handling the fact that he was laid off three weeks ago and has not yet found another job. In a unique way he has been drawing on God's varied resources to carry him and his family through this pressure period. You know the rest of the congregation would profit from hearing Dan and you ask him to share these insights next Sunday in the evening service. He agrees. But Sunday evening is a disaster. Dan is afraid of the mike and doesn't use it. His soft voice barely makes it to the first row. He leaves out two-thirds of what he told you, and the third he presents is disorganized and rambling. Your response? "I'll never do that again."

Wait a minute! Before you throw in the testimony towel, try the interview method. What you really want is to duplicate the conversation you and Dan had over lunch on Tuesday. You can accomplish that by interviewing Dan on Sunday evening. Put a lapel mike on him. Have him sit on a stool or an easy chair across from you on the platform, and in a casual interview draw out the insights he shared with you.

People enjoy listening to a conversation, especially when it contains personal details about individuals, differing points of view, and humor. Interviewing allows you to tap one or more of these areas. Here are some ways to use the interview method:

- New believers—incidents and individuals that God used in their conversion experience.
- New members—who are they? Where do they come from? What do they do? Why did they choose this church?
- Missionaries—candidates on deputation, those on home assignment. Their work, their needs, their plans, their frustrations.

- College or seminary students home on vacation—their studies, future plans.
- New leaders in the church—their gifts, their goals.
- Special occasions—anniversaries, moving away, graduation, engagement, marriage, short-term missionaries, retirement, etc.

These kinds of interviews could be integrated into sermons or stand alone in other parts of the service.

Don't stop with the foregoing suggestions. Put your creative imagination to work. Starting a series on Galatians? In your first message interview the author—the apostle Paul. Ask him why he wrote the letter, where he was at the time, to whom he wrote it, how he is getting along with Peter, how he feels about the Galatians, what prompted him to use such strong language in 3:1, what he did for three years in Arabia (1:17), and why he calls attention to his writing in 6:11. This method will allow you to cover what is often pedantic introductory material in an interesting, unusual way.

You could use the same technique with reference to any biblical character—about a particular experience he or she had which is recorded in Scripture, or about a lesson learned, a decision made, a truth presented, or what was really meant in a given verse of Scripture.

Now and then make a secondhand illustration your own by using an interview approach. Betty related an incident during the week that beautifully illustrates a point you are going to make in your sermon. Instead of telling the congregation what she said, pause and interact with her right there in the sanctuary during the sermon. You can dialogue between pulpit and pew, or you can ask her to come up to the platform and interact with her there, putting her at a microphone to be sure she is heard by everyone. All this, of course, would be planned ahead and rehearsed.

Here are some hints for better interviewing. Don't preface your questions with unnecessary words such as "Let me ask you a question." Ask simple, specific questions:

"How were you saved?" is too complex and too general; "What incident did God first use to make you aware of your spiritual need?" is simple and singular.

Use both fact and feeling questions. "When did you get married?" "Who told you it was wrong?" These are fact questions; ask plenty of them. "How did you know you were in love?" "How did you react when you found out it was wrong?" These are feeling questions; ask plenty of them too.

The interviewees are an important party to this dialogue. They should answer questions briefly and to the point. Draw out more detail with further questions. If you ask, "Where were you born?" and they proceed to give their life history, dialogue shuts down and you lose the dynamic of a good interview. Last but not least, even though an interview can and should have freshness and spontaneity, it should be rehearsed; and it is perfectly acceptable to use notes.

PRINTED MATERIALS

A skeletal sermon outline in the bulletin will prompt many people to follow the sermon more closely and take notes. A complete outline gives them more detail but less incentive to write. Some "fill-in-the-blank" outlines may stimulate more active involvement. How about a pre-sermon quiz in the bulletin to whet their appetite for what is coming, or to test their knowledge of the subject or their attitudes toward it? You might try a question in the bulletin for people to ponder before the message, or a teaser question or interest-catching statement in this week's bulletin for next week's sermon.

Develop a brief set of agree/disagree statements that relate to today's or next week's sermon, or a diagram that graphically relates to the sermon topic—for example, a teeter-totter drawn in the bulletin each Sunday for a series on living the balanced life. Have you tried a practical application assignment printed up and passed out to members of the congregation as they leave, designed for discussion at the noon meal or to be used in personal devotions during the week? Maps, charts, stimulating or controversial quotes, sermon synopses, and the like can also be printed.

Here are some guidelines for using print media. Keep the material simple and uncluttered. (It helps if your sermon also has those characteristics.) Refer to printed helps. Encourage use of them. Don't assume people love to read and write. Stimulate writing and preserving by furnishing Bible-sized (4¼ x 5½) punched notes, loose-leaf notebooks, and different colored paper for different series.

SECURING FEEDBACK

We continue to suffer from what Reuel Howe calls the "monological illusion."[2] The illusion is that communication is accomplished by telling people what they ought to know. Discussion and feedback greatly facilitate the preacher's awareness of what has actually been communicated and what people want and need to know. Sunday evening is a good time and place to discuss the meaning and implications of the morning message. You can use individual reactors or a reaction panel immediately after the sermon.

I once asked our head usher if he would ask two persons to be ready to ask two key questions after the sermon. I told him not to tell me who they were. At the close of this message I informed the audience that two of them were primed to respond. They did—putting me on the spot!

Discussion questions can be given to people to take home and use. After a message, the congregation can be divided into small groups, and right there in the sanctuary a guided discussion of the message can be organized. If your Sunday school meets after the service, consider having the classes discuss the sermon. At that point you will have what every educator wants—prepared pupils! You can also appoint certain people to give you written or oral feedback on the message; they become your sermon response team. A card in the pew racks or a tear-off in the bulletin will allow anyone to give you their perspective on the message.

It is even in the realm of possibility to have Sunday school classes that meet before the worship service to do some preliminary study in the text to be preached. Or you might have a "Sermon Discussion Class" that meets periodically or regularly either before or after the worship service to allow those who wish to discuss the message they are going to hear or have just heard. The preacher can conduct this, or any qualified teacher can do it. Keep this thought in mind: you are always stimulating feedback when you preach. The only question is, is it harnessed and healthy and being heard by you and others who need to hear it, or is it going underground as gossip?

DIALOGUE PREACHING

Two people, preferably you being one of them, can study a passage of Scripture together, prepare a sermon together, and preach it together. The team can alternate on words, phrases, clauses, or verses. One can handle the observation phase, the other providing the interpretation. One could illustrate, and the other deal with application. One can challenge the interpretation, the other can defend it. You can both use the same pulpit, but it is better to have separate speaker's stands. It is probably best to sit on stools or chairs and clear the platform of the large pulpit and other furniture that may be in the way.

If dialogue preaching is to succeed, there must be good preparation, and dynamic, aggressive interaction. Though you can use notes, there needs to be a spontaneity to the presentation. In other words, be natural and be professional. This method is a fine way to train younger staff members and laypeople to preach. You have the experience in preaching, so you can ensure that the presentation does not bog down or get off the track. The dynamics of dialogue will allow you to use a lot of natural humor, yet in the same message you can be deeply serious.

On occasion I have shortened a dialogue sermon and used the last ten minutes for questions and comments from the audience. Dialogue preaching will also facilitate using a resource person who has insights in certain areas germane to the text. For example, I once had a dialogue with a counselor in an exposition of the story of the Prodigal Son (Luke 15:11–32). I developed the theological aspects and he handled the psychological. We spent hours going over this passage together. The intense preparation paid off.

DRAMATIZING THE BIBLE AND DOCTRINE

Dramatic potential resides in many portions of the Scriptures. The scripts need not be long and complex. All that is required is a fairly fertile imagination and some time. For instance, everybody in your church listens to news on the radio. Why not present a portion of the Bible framed in this format? Tune in and listen to an example.

Drama in Daniel

Ann:

You are listening to the number one station in Babylon—KNEB—with studios atop the Shinar Sheraton in beautiful downtown Babylon—serving the greater Tigris and Euphrates valleys.

The time on our Mesopotamian moondial is now 7:30 in the evening.

The following announcement is brought to you as a public service by this station in cooperation with the Babylonian Big Brothers and the Chaldean Community Chest.

The Big Brothers and the Community Chest are sponsoring a benefit barbecue and chariot show at the local fairgrounds tomorrow evening from five until ten. Food will be served during the entire time. As you eat delicious meat roasted over coals from the finest Lebanese logs, you may wander through the magnificent display of chariots. You will see the newest in styles and the latest ideas in design. Don't miss the slick wheels, padded dash, disc brakes, suspension ride, bucket seats. And there will be free chariot rides for all the children. All this for just ten shekels for adults and five shekels for children. All proceeds go to help the Babylonian Big Brothers and the Chaldean Community Chest. Don't miss this exciting evening and the opportunity to help these worthy projects.

You've just finished a meal of tasty trout from the Tigris—and you're comfortable—with KNEB.

So now—for the latest news—here's our man of the hour with news up to the minute—Haul Parvey.

Haul:

Hello, Babylonians—this is Haul Parvey!

A chariot was hijacked three hours ago on route 666 just west of the city. Two men drew their swords and ordered the driver to change his course and take them to Macedonia. It is suspected that these men are wise men from King Nebuchadnezzar's court and that they are seeking to find asylum in a neutral country.

This is just one of the many exciting events that have been occurring all day long since the execution edict was issued by the king this morning. As you know, earlier today the king issued a command that all the court-appointed wise men of the nation were to be taken into custody and be put to death. This order was prompted by the failure of this group to reveal to the king both the content and meaning of a strange dream he recently had. Special agents from the palace security force have been rounding up all the wise men throughout the country. The date of execution will be announced soon. This station will carry the event live.

And now here's a bulletin just handed me direct from the palace press secretary: "The order to execute the wise men has been temporarily suspended by the king. The occasion for such action is to allow one of the wise men—a young Jew named Belteshazzar—to see if he can explain the dream to the king. The king has allowed him forty-eight hours to secure the needed information. In the meantime, no wise men will be allowed to leave the country." What a fascinating story! Be sure and stay tuned to this station for the latest developments as they occur. Haul Parvey . . . good day!

This drama, based on Daniel 2, was designed to highlight the contents of the chapter through a contemporary medium, radio. Two offstage voices presented this material, after which I reinforced the broadcast with an exposition of the text itself.

On another occasion I was preaching on the passage concerning demons in Mark 1:25–28. I wanted to give the congregation an orientation to these nefarious characters. I wrote the script and enlisted a young man with a high-pitched voice to dialogue with me on Sunday. He was at an offstage mike and I was standing at the pulpit. I made my beginning statement and he came screeching through the speakers. I focused my attention on the speakers and we went at it, providing the people with a short course on biblical demonology.

An Interview With Dirk the Demon

P: I don't know about you, but I'm always a bit leery of something that actually exists, yet I can't see it.

D: That doesn't bother me one bit.

P: Well, who are you?

D: Well, I guess I am the kind of thing you are talking about. I exist, but you can't see me.

P: I can certainly *hear* you. Who did you say you are?

D: I'm Dirk—Dirk the Demon. I hang around here quite a lot.

P: Are you especially assigned to public address systems? I'll bet you're the one who puts the hum in the speakers, burns out the amplifiers, blows the fuses, loosens the connections . . .

D: Look—I'm in the business of fouling up the communication of the Word of God. But I must say, there are usually enough dum-dum Christians botching it up so well, there's little left for me to do. You know—preachers and teachers who aren't well-prepared, material that is poorly presented, someone who forgets to turn on the microphone, connections that are half-soldered . . . Christians are getting so sloppy—bless their hearts—I love 'em!

P: Where did you come from?

D: Heaven. You might say I'm one of those individuals who started at the top, and I'm working my way down. I used to be an angel . . .

P: An angel?

D: Yeh—an angel! Just sitting around strumming and singing and serving. Then I got involved in the ACLU.

P: The ACLU?

D: Right—the Angels Celestial Liberties Union. A bunch of us got together and decided we didn't want *Him* to run the whole show. Our celestial rights were being violated. So we started planning a revolution.

P: What happened?

D: Man, what a counterintelligence system *He's* got! We were discovered before we hardly got going—and we were thrown out. I'm still trying to figure out how *He* knew what we were thinking . . .

P: So you used to be an angel in heaven, but you were thrown out because you were trying to take over?

D: That's right! Kicked out! Leader and all. Sent to earth, of all places! But our leader is something else—he just transferred the revolt to this scene, and we have been giving the Man Upstairs fits ever since.

P: How many demons are there?

D: Sorry, I can't tell you! That's—uh—classified information. But believe me, you can't count that high.

P: Well now! Just what do you do?

D: Simple! I do everything possible to get people to leave *Him* out. Sometimes I make people miserable—and then I sit back and watch them blame *Him*. Or frequently I make people real happy and prosperous—so they figure they don't need *Him*. You know, I really get a thrill out of my work—devising ways to stimulate people to revolt against *Him*.

P: Has your approach changed down through the years?

D: Oh my, yes! We used to move in and completely dominate a person's life—take over and make them act like we wanted them to.

P: That's probably what we call demon possession. Do you still do that?

D: We sure do. In some places we can control a few superstitious souls and get them so scared and confused they'll worship anything. But in places like _____ [name of town] where people are educated, cultured, religious, and some are even Christians, we have developed a more subtle approach. We've got a system that is absolutely satanic—if you'll pardon the expression. We infiltrate life with R.M.N.

P: R.M.N.? What does that stand for?

D: Rationalism . . . Materialism . . . Naturalism. We have filtered these ideas into every area of society. And, boy, is it working! People are convinced that they are smart enough to solve all their problems—that's rationalism. They worship money and possessions—that's materialism. And they are sure that supernatural things don't happen—that's naturalism.

P: But does that make people revolt against God?

D: Well, it sure doesn't make them bow down before *Him!* It just makes them happy without *Him.* And that's what we want—a pleasant revolution!

P: Dirk, you seem so positive and confident. Even a bit cocky, I'd say! As if the revolution is successful. The world is yours.

D: It is! It is! We try harder! We're number one!

P: Aren't you afraid of anything?

D: Only one person—*Him.* We're all afraid of *Him.* You can study the first chapter of the Gospel of Mark and understand why.

P: That's exactly what we intend to do. Right now! How about staying around and studying it with us?

D: No way! I've got more important things to do! There are some of your people who are still in bed. I'm going to confirm in their minds that they are right where they ought to be . . .

This drama was presented in a fairly formal Sunday morning worship service. Those who were expecting the norm were a bit startled, but by that time I had been there for seven years, and they trusted me. They knew that even when my methodology was unpredictably creative, my theology was still soundly conservative!

The Bible oozes with dramatic possibilities. Want to deal with conflict? Let Paul and Barnabas get into the act (Acts 15). Want to give your people insight on Bible study and teaching/preaching? Walk them through the entire sermon-building process instead of giving them the product.

CREATIVITY IN PREACHING

Want to appeal to every age? Let a puppet rise out of the baptistry and comment on your sermon. Need insight on failure? Talk with Peter. Or be Peter and talk to yourself. Want perspective on sovereignty? Chat with Nebuchadnezzar. Interested in finding out how Satan operates? Interview Job. Want to know more about heaven? Consult an angel— Michael, for instance. Dealing with the fall of man? Contact Adam and Eve.

You may not be strong in seeing these possibilities, nor strong in putting them into effect. If you still want to explore the potential, look for those in your congregation who are willing and able.

IN SUMMARY

We all gravitate toward certain preaching methods and preaching styles. It is in these areas we are comfortable and reasonably successful. We ought to identify them and use them often, constantly striving to raise our level of excellence.

A growing preacher, however, should also be exploring other ways of communicating truth, not to replace the tried and true, but to expand one's God-given potential. Sometimes the poorest method is the one we use all the time, simply because we may start taking it for granted and become a bit sloppy, or because we start to become predictable. This chapter has been written to challenge you to be a little less predictable by being a little more creative.

7

Creative Use
of Visual Aids
in Preaching

Seeing adds a vital dimension to the communication process. Your congregation usually sees the pulpit, your Bible, and you. The size and substance of the pulpit, as well as the amount of roaming that you do while you are preaching, will determine how much they see of you. Your body language will add further visual messages. It would be wise periodically to have your preaching videotaped and see what others see when you preach. The camera does not lie.

OBJECT LESSONS

There are as many object lessons as there are objects. Bringing an object into the pulpit to display and use at the opportune time will enhance your communication and reinforce your appeal to people's sense of sight. There are numerous good object-lesson books; stop by the bookstore and buy one. Enlist the aid of others in your congregation who may have skill with visual aids.

Suppose you are preaching on commitment in marriage from a passage such as Genesis 2:24. What object lesson could you use? Go to your toolbox and find two small, different-shaped pieces of wood, then clamp them together with a "C-clamp." During the sermon use the object lesson to point out that there are numerous external pressures that push couples into engagement and marriage, such as peer pressure, parents, pregnancy, infatuation, or desperation. After you have been married for a while, these pressures tend to drop off (remove the clamp), and what is *between* holds you together. If it is a superficial commitment, you can easily drift apart. If it is a deep, genuine, loving commitment, you will stick with each other and work out your difficulties in the light of your mutual commitment. (If you want to focus on a superficial, externally oriented commitment, don't glue the pieces of wood together; if you want to emphasize an internally oriented commitment, do glue.)

How about an object lesson to illustrate your philosophy of preaching? Obtain an empty, opaque, plastic bleach bottle. Put an inch or two of dirt in it and screw the cap on. Hold it up and ask each member of the congregation to think of himself or herself as one of these small-necked bottles. Your preaching task is to insert biblical truth into the person (bottle). People can help by being open and ready to receive truth (removing their "caps") and by ridding themselves of their sin through confession and cleansing. (As you say these words, unscrew the cap and pour out the dirt.)

Now comes the preaching. Your challenge is to get a lot of truth into every person. At this point lift a large tub of water, telling the congregation that you want to fill all the bottles with "truth" with one flip of the tub. (Demonstrate your tub-flipping technique.) Alas, you can't do it! The openings are too small. Most of the "truth" will deceptively run down the outside of the bottles and end up on the floor. The solution is not more "truth tubs" or bigger bottles. The solution is to fill an *eyedropper* with water from the tub and walk among the bottles—giving each person an individualized, internal injection of truth from God's Word. That's your philosophy of personalized preaching and, incidentally, the congregation's philosophy of personalized listening.

Preaching on John 15? Bring a vine into the pulpit.

Expounding on James 1:22–25? Use a mirror. Dealing with Hebrews 10:24? Consider having a pair of spurs or a cattle prod. Handling Hebrews 5:11–14? Drink a glass of milk and eat a raw carrot—during the sermon. Then explain that what the milk and carrot do for you physically, the Word of God will do for you spiritually. Incidentally, explaining the latter point will not be as easy as you might think.

Are you getting the picture? There are object lessons right in the text as well as beyond the text. Look for both. Set a goal: an object lesson in a sermon at least once a month.

OVERHEAD PROJECTION

The overhead projector allows us to project things on the screen without turning off the lights or losing eye contact with our congregation. How can we use this visual aid in our preaching? Everything that we can print in the bulletin, we can also print on a transparency and project onto the screen. Quizzes, quotes, agree/disagree statements, outlines, verses of Scripture, key words and phrases, cross references, theme or proposition statements, questions, case studies, "What would you do?" situations, and more.

For example, as people sit in the sanctuary waiting for the service to start, their thinking could be stimulated and directed by a quote on the screen that reads:

"When Christians don't suffer, the church does."

Pondering this statement would help prepare the congregation to listen carefully to a sermon that will explain it.[1] Or, on the lighter side, a message on faith and doubt could be focused in a word picture like this:

"Doubts are ants in the pants of faith."[2]

This is a totally different way of expressing truth. It has a bite to it. It will sting you into involvement. Or another:

"Always pray about a matter before you talk to anyone else about it." Agree? Disagree?

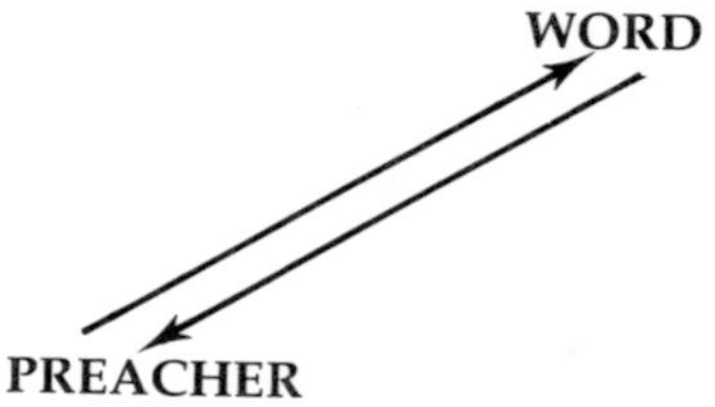

WORD

PREACHER

Figure 7.1

Etch truth into the minds of people not only by the sermons you preach, but also by the short, pithy statements you project on the screen that boil your sermon down into a few choice words.

Graphics—vivid visual ways of showing significant relationships and responsibilities—can and should occasionally be used in your preaching. Lines, circles, arrows, and boxes, along with key words, are effective ways of depicting concepts, organization, order, structure, integration, separation, dependency, interdependency, sequence, origin, and other concepts. For example, the two arrows in figure 7.1 convey the concept that the task of the preacher is twofold—to get into the Word and to let the Word get into him.

These two responsibilities demand study and an openness to God on the part of the preacher. If you are not strong in both, your preaching will be weak, shallow, and superficial. In figure 7.2 we add two more arrows that show that the preacher is also to get into the lives of his congregation and let them get into his life.

Getting into the Word and letting the Word get into you require an ongoing desire to get to know others, and a willingness to let them get to know you. If you are not strong in both, your preaching will be at best theoretical; at worst, sterile. Finally, in figure 7.3 we add two more arrows to indicate that the congregation is to get into the Word and allow the Word to get into their experience.

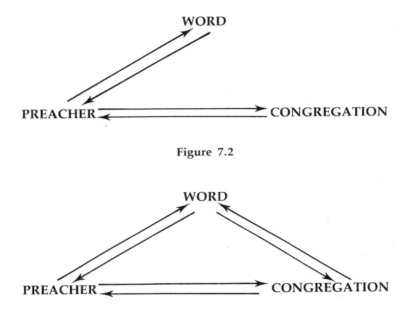

Figure 7.2

Figure 7.3

These two responsibilities can only be accomplished when you decide that your congregation must learn how to study and apply the Bible on their own, instead of just learning how to listen to the results of your study of the Word. Three key words and six significant arrows have been employed to visually articulate a biblical philosophy of preaching—in fact, a biblical philosophy of ministry. A simple diagram. A significant and complex idea. Our temptation is to clutter up important biblical concepts with a lot of verbiage. Simplify! Good visual aids will help.

Remember, you are a person, preaching to persons. One of the best ways to personalize your preaching is to project people onto the screen. All kinds of people: men and women, young and old, happy and sad, black and white.

Give them names. Focus on their faces. Portray different *facial expressions,* because each facial expression arises out of, and gives evidence for, a particular life-setting.

Consider Tom and Cheryl, a typical couple in their mid-thirties (fig. 7.4). Cheryl is a homemaker, has two grade-school children, and works two nights a week as a nurse at a local hospital. Tom is an accountant who is with a group, but is thinking seriously of going into business for himself. They met in college and were married after graduation.

Figure 7.4

In a sermon you could project Tom and Cheryl onto the screen and give your congregation biographical data like that given above. Adapt the information to your setting. If they live in a rural community, you might want to change the description. Your main purpose is to relate the text you are preaching to the life-setting of this couple. They appear happy—and it could be because they are applying this truth to their lives. You may wish to elaborate on this condition.

Tom is contemplating a major job-change decision. Could the truth of the text be related to this decision?

Cheryl is gone two nights a week from the house. Is this a truth that could tie in with the fulfillment she experiences as a nurse? Could it relate to the fact that Tom bought a fancy sports car and that is one of the main reasons Cheryl had to go back to work?

Are Tom and Cheryl happy in particular areas of their

marriage? If so, is it because they have been putting this truth into practice? Do they just look happy, when in fact they aren't, and is it all a façade? Is it because they are ignorant of this truth? Or could it be that they know it, but aren't doing it?

Obviously you don't try to force the text into all these matters, but seek to interpret and apply it where it clearly impinges on life. While you are carrying on this life-setting preaching, adding visual impact to your verbal presentation, members of your congregation are with you, not only because of what you are saying, but also because of whom they are seeing. In various ways they are identifying with Tom and/or Cheryl. The younger ones are headed in that direction in their experience, and you are prompting them to think about what they should do now to ensure a positive future for them and their marriage. Others are right where Tom and Cheryl are now; from the Word you can give them insight they can use immediately. The older ones are looking back, and with a seasoned maturity they are thinking about how they made some of the same mistakes and solved some of the same kinds of problems by applying God's truth to their lives. Putting Tom and Cheryl on the screen, even for a moment, will enhance the ability to relate the truth to life.

This is Charlie (fig. 7.5). What is he reading? Perhaps a layoff notice, an unexpected bill, a letter of rejection, a lower grade than he anticipated. Suggest to your congregation a number of options.

Life is like this. We all get bad news. Your sermon may be along the lines of John 16:33, helping people accept the reality of problems. Or it may be a text such as Philippians 4:6–7, helping people to realize the

Figure 7.5

101

power of prayer. Using these texts gives the impression that what has happened was not Charlie's fault. It could have been, and you may want to explore that avenue with a passage such as Galatians 6:7–8.

Visuals can help in *application*. You have expounded the truth of a given text and now you intend to mount a full-scale invasion into the lives of your people. You could say these words, or have someone else (visible or hidden) say them, or put them on the screen (see fig. 7.6).

> "If that's what the Word of God says, and if that's what it means, and if it is really true, and I believe it is, then I think I had better start making some changes."

"Good thinking, Fred. Now, based on this truth, what specific things can you start doing this week in your relationship to your customers and fellow employees at the office?"

"You are right on target, Norma. How would these biblical imperatives affect your attitude toward your invalid husband and those rambunctious grandchildren?"

Figure 7.6

You could furnish these answers yourself, or you could draw them from a Fred and Norma offstage. You might make a suggestion and have one or both of them disagree and offer something much more pertinent to their respective

Figure 7.7

situations. In the final analysis, you want to inject truth into their life-settings and to train them to do it on their own. To do this you may have to come across as someone who doesn't have all the answers. What a blow!

Occupations are another crucial area (fig. 7.7). Your people spend forty hours a week at their jobs. What they do is important. How they do it is also important. Give your people names: Sheila Secretary, Bert Builder. Then relate the Word to the importance of their jobs and to the quality of their work. How do they feel about what they are doing? What does it mean for each of them to be successful? How can they witness on the job? What pressures are there to be sloppy, slow, dishonest? What potential for advancement is there? Can what they are doing be classified as "the Lord's work"?

Be sure to use pictures that can be related to members of your congregation. The visuals in figure 7.7 are quite relevant to the building trades or office work. To touch other people you might depict, or at least refer to, Boss Barney, who supervises Bert's carpentry, or Banker Bill, who puts up the money for the entire project. Sheila may work for Manager Maude—who normally is a teddy bear but now and then a tyrant. It is your privilege as the preacher to bring the truth of the Word into the world where your people work.

Figure 7.8

Overlays give us the chance to develop a *sequence*. That's the way we live, in sequence, constantly processing data from within and beyond ourselves and then responding with our thoughts, feelings, and actions.

Here is Sensitive Steve (fig. 7.8). In scene 1, he doesn't look too happy. Why not? A customer just worked him over on the phone for not delivering an order on time. It caught Steve off guard, and his immediate reaction was to be miserable, mad, and sad. He might be saying things to himself like "It's not my fault, it's the shipping department's" or "That's the third time this week this has happened; I can't seem to do anything right."

You might ask your congregation to come up with words and phrases that could describe what is going on inside Steve. They know. They've been there.

Now project the second panel onto the screen, overlapping the first illustration. The facial expression and the size of the cloud would indicate that Steve is mulling his way through this experience in a fairly healthy, positive way. Could that be because he is bringing the Word of God into this situation? It certainly could be. As a matter of fact, it could be the very portion of Scripture on which you are preaching. The Scriptures say something about making promises you can't keep; about dealing with people who are angry and overbearing; about learning from adversity.

Next comes panel 3, overlapping the others: the sun is shining and Steve is smiling. How long did it take him to work his way through these issues? A few moments, a number of hours, maybe all day, or even all week. But he was sensitive enough to relate the Word of God to his life-setting, and that's what you want your people to be able to do. Are you equipping them to do that? Do you see how pictures will help?

Steve came through his experience with flying colors and ended up with a smile on his face. It doesn't always work like that. Sometimes matters go from bad to worse. Meet my friend, Gloria, for instance. I call her "Gloomy Gloria," because she tends to turn numerous negative facts loose in her mind. As they roam around inside her, they not only bruise her ego, but also tend to color her outlook on life—at best, blue; at worst, black.

In the first scene (fig. 7.9) you can see a cloud with a somber lining beginning to form. Why? Gloria is thinking of the never-ending demands placed upon her to be a gorgeous wife and a model mother. In scene 2 she adds to her list the challenge of being a gourmet cook and an efficient house-keeper. The cloud gets bigger, lower, darker; the look on her face, more perplexed. In scene 3 she ponders the probability that she will never get to engage in the med-tech career she was trained for. Living with unfulfilled desires and dreams can be frustrating and depressing, especially when you are a perfectionist, as Gloria is.

Preacher, like it or not, you are ministering to people like Gloria. Once in a while, expound on a text that will allow

Figure 7.9

you to visualize and relate to the three phases of Gloria's depression. Do this, and I guarantee that you will have the rapt attention of every woman in your congregation. They will not only listen to you, but also identify with Gloria—and they will be looking for answers from the Word of God. Furthermore, you will reach the men in your audience, for they will be asking themselves two prime questions: "What am I doing to foster this depression?" and "What can I do to help?" Give them answers.

Then there is Stressed-out Sam (fig. 7.10). (Or it could be Burned-out Becky? Women are not immune from pressure.) Every day Sam plays this game called "Perfection." He shuffles the cards, cuts the deck, and deals himself a hand, hoping to get the cards labeled "Be everywhere," "Know everything," "Do everything," "Judge everyone," "Equip everyone." He never seems to draw these cards, but being the driven person that he is, he has fine-tuned his "bluffing"

Figure 7.10

skills and plays a mean game of perfection, even though, in his infrequent moments of rational thinking, he knows it's not in the cards for himself or anyone else.

What biblical principles is Sam violating to get himself into this mode of thinking and living? What biblical insights would help him lower his tension and frenzy? What do people who live with him and work with him need? Everyone experiences stress. The picture above may over-state the condition of a person under a lot of stress, but it is so graphic it will get everyone's attention. We magnify the problem in order to facilitate evaluation and solution.

Here are some guidelines for overhead projection. It is a powerful visual aid, so use it. Don't use it all the time, lest you become too dependent on it and too predictable with it. Buy a good screen; position it so that it can be seen by everyone without a "keystone" distortion. Secure a good overhead projector; put it on a stand that is solid and the right height. Furnish and arrange your platform and pulpit so that the projector is not an unsightly intrusion. Look for people in your church who have artistic or graphics interests or experience. Recruit them and use them. Secure the basic equipment you need to make quality transparencies—qual-ity in color and design. The world around us is profuse with quality media. Don't let your church go second-rate. Even if you can't start with high quality, aim toward it.

IN CONCLUSION

There are many, many more creative things you can do with the overhead projector, and other visual aids. We have mentioned a few and purposefully tied them in with our life-setting perspective. If you aren't using visual aids regularly, you ought to change. The preaching ministry is too significant for us to set narrow, rigid limits on how we preach. People and their cultures are too diverse for us to assume there is one best way to communicate truth to them. And finally, each preacher is so unique that it is a tragedy for him not to discover, develop, and use this God-given uniqueness creatively in his own preaching.

Epilogue

This is a book about preaching.

About preaching creatively.

This is a book about life-settings.

About discovering and using them.

This book says that good preaching will . . .

creatively re-create the life-setting of the text,
creatively relate to the life-setting of the congregation,
creatively use the life-setting of the preacher, and
creatively employ life-setting preaching methods.

This book says that you can be a more creative preacher.

If you want to.
If you work at it.

This book will probably cause one of the following responses:

Resignation: "Not me."
Procrastination: "Not now."
Consecration: "I'll do it."

This book has gone as far as it can go.

Now it's up to you.

Notes

Chapter 1

1. *2 Corinthians 5:18–21:* "All this" would relate to the *truth* in the text about being a new creation in Christ. The reality of this truth is "from God." "Who reconciled us to himself through Christ" is also part of the *text* to be proclaimed. It is a clear, simple statement of the message of reconciliation. "Gave us" emphasizes the preachers who were assigned the task of preaching. "The ministry of reconciliation" stresses the preaching, with "ministry" (Gr., *diakonian*) giving attention to the loving activity of the preacher as a servant.

"That God was reconciling the world to himself in Christ, not counting men's sins against them"—an enlarged restatement of the *text*, i.e., the message of reconciliation. Note, however, that here "he has committed to us the *message* of reconciliation." Message (Gr., *logon*) underscores the importance of the text. The preacher is an "ambassador" who communicates important messages (*texts*) to those in other countries. He seeks to present and explain (*preach*) as clearly and as accurately as he can. "Making his appeal through us" combines the preacher and his preaching, as does also "we implore you." Verse 21 is a climaxing, reconfirming condensation of the message of the text.

Chapter 2

1. See Acts 14:15; 17:24–28; Colossians 1:15–17, and 2 Peter 3:1–16 for further insights on God as creator, sustainer, and re-creator.

2. See the author's book *The Trauma of Transparency* (Portland, Oreg.: Multnomah, 1979), ch. 1, for additional thoughts on the relationship between Adam and Eve before the Fall.

Notes

3. Richard F. Lovelace, *Renewal as a Way of Life* (Downers Grove, Ill.: InterVarsity, 1985), pp. 75–76. Lovelace has three excellent chapters on the world, the flesh, and the devil.

Chapter 3

1. Paul L. Kaufman, *An Introductory Grammar of New Testament Greek* (Palm Springs, Calif.: Ronald N. Haynes, 1982), p. 136.

2. Ibid., p. 32. For further insight on the different uses of *ex* as a prefix, see A. T. Robertson, *A Grammar of the Greek New Testament in the Light of Historical Research* (Nashville: Broadman, 1934). The terms *artios* and *exertismenos* are discussed in *The New International Dictionary of New Testament Theology*, ed. Colin Brown (Grand Rapids: Zondervan, 1978), 3:350.

3. Here are some data for you. The couplets in 2 Corinthians 4:8–9 are instructive. Note the intensifying prefix that moves one from perplexity to despair. The power of God will keep that from happening (4:7). The double prefixed word in Romans 15:32 will help you better to understand Paul's concept of how believers rejuvenate and refresh one another. It seems redundant to add *syn* before *koinoneo* as Paul did in Philippians 4:14. Why would he have done this?

4. See the author's book *The Trauma of Transparency* (Portland, Oreg.: Multnomah, 1979), ch. 8, for insight on "Communicating With Yourself."

Chapter 4

1. Henri J. M. Nouwen, *The Wounded Healer* (Garden City, N.Y.: Doubleday, 1972).

2. For additional information on using laypeople in sermon preparation and evaluation, see Reuel L. Howe, *Partners in Preaching* (New York: Seabury, 1967).

Chapter 5

1. IDAK Research Associates, Inc., has developed a simple *Talent Discovery Guide* and a more detailed *Career Match*, both of which are designed to help people discover their God-given talents. For information, write IDAK, 7931 N.E. Halsey, Portland, OR 97213.

2. See Myron R. Chartier, *Preaching as Communication* (Nashville: Abingdon, 1981). Chapter 2 contains an excellent treatment of "Self-disclosure in Preaching." I recommend that the entire book be read by every preacher.

Chapter 6

1. Charlotte I. Lee, *Oral Reading of the Scriptures.* (Boston: Houghton Mifflin, 1974). The author provides insights for the public oral reading of the Scriptures with attention to their different literary styles.

2. Reuel L. Howe, *The Miracle of Dialogue* (New York: Seabury, 1963), p. 32.

Chapter 7

1. This is a sermon based on Philippians 1:27–30. The thrust is that the church is supposed to prepare its people to live in the world in such a way that they may have to suffer hostility, rejection, and so on. The same church is then available to help us when we do suffer. But when Christians don't suffer, the church does. It suffers from a lack of purpose and a failure to do what it is supposed to do. It is existing, but not ministering; therefore it is suffering.

2. Frederick Buechner, *Wishful Thinking—A Theological ABC* (New York: Harper & Row, 1973), p. 20. A theological dictionary with brief, pithy definitions of many biblical terms and theological concepts.